# POEMS BY
# FAIZ

# اِنتساب

بیگم ایلس فیض کے نام

TO

ALYS FAIZ AHMED

# POEMS BY

# FAIZ

## Faiz Ahmed Faiz

*Translated, with an*
*Introduction and Notes by*
V.G. KIERNAN

# اِنتخابِ فیض

نقشِ فریادی، دستِ صبا، زِندان نامہ اور دستِ تہِ سنگ
کی
مُنتخب غزلوں اور نظموں کا مجموعہ

وِکٹر کِرنان
اُستادِ جامعۂ ایڈنبرا
کے
منظوم انگریزی ترجمے کے ساتھ

خطاطی: [illegible] (پاکستان)

OXFORD
UNIVERSITY PRESS

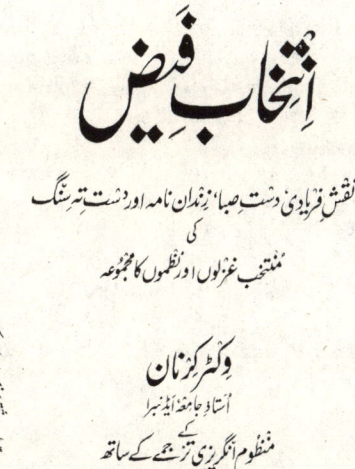

OXFORD
UNIVERSITY PRESS

Oxford University Press is a department of the University of Oxford. It furthers the University's objective of excellence in research, scholarship, and education by publishing worldwide. Oxford is a registered trademark of Oxford University Press in the UK and in certain other countries

Published in India by
Oxford University Press
22 Workspace, 2nd Floor, 1/22 Asaf Ali Road, New Delhi 110 002, India



First Edition published in 1971
Oxford India Paperbacks 2000
37th impression 2025



ISBN-13: 978-0-19-565198-0
ISBN-10: 0-19-565198-7

Printed in India by Replika Press Pvt. Ltd

# PREFACE TO THE PAPERBACK EDITION

Faiz was much influenced by his forerunner Ghalib, and between them the two may be said to mark the beginning and the end of a golden age, a century and a half of Urdu poetry. What they had in common, apart from genius, was that each belonged to a society whose outlook on life was fading, and which compelled them to open their windows to the outer world. Ghalib belonged to the twilight court of the Mughal emperors at Delhi, but he travelled far enough to see Calcutta, a modern city founded by the Europeans. Faiz belonged to the Punjab, and its capital Lahore, which was in his time still an intriguing blend of medieval and modern, ruled by a partnership of feudal landlords and British governors. He too was to visit Calcutta, as well as places even further, as remote as Addis Ababa, London, and Honolulu. Both Ghalib and Faiz heard voices calling to them from the outer world; the voice heard by Faiz was that of Karl Marx.

Faiz never lost touch with his native corner of the countryside, but when I got to know him, at the end of the thirties, he was a junior college teacher—of English and Arabic, symbolic perhaps of dual origins—first in Amritsar and then in Lahore. As a writer he came to the fore early. He and others of his time were assisted by the radio, then just being inaugurated; their recitations were a favourite item with listeners, especially poems that could be set to music and sung by professionals.

The war began, the end of the empire was suddenly approaching, Faiz and his generation felt both excitement and hope, especially after the USSR was brought into the conflict by Hitler. Independence came, in 1947, but it was clouded by the manner of its coming. Life in what had suddenly become a new country, which had not yet found itself, might well have brought with it feelings of isolation and abandonment. Poem no. 8, 'Solitude', is based on an old theme in the Persian tradition, but Faiz gives it new meaning. Hopes of change and progress, such as may be found in no. 31, were often dashed. Yet his prison poems are among his very best. Heinrich Heine (1797–1856) spoke for many poets in his lines:

'Out of my heavy griefs I make my little songs.'

Peace in our twentieth century, so full of mankind's self-inflicted sufferings, was another ideal quickly blighted. It is finely expressed in no. 39, the gift of a visit to Sinkiang. At this moment in the year 2000, alas, the war-drums are beating as fiercely as ever on Faiz's frontiers.

A letter from our joint friend Dr Nazir Ahmad, the highly respected Principal of Government College, in April 1970, told me of rabid abuse of Faiz from religious fanatics, so outrageous that a murderous attack on him could well be feared. At that time Faiz was doing good in a quiet way by serving as an adviser on education in the occupied part of Kashmir; but he had been seen at socialist meetings, and that was enough for the bigots.

He was not an armchair reformer, but a pioneer ready to take part in any ongoing efforts for progress. He took risks, and encountered many disappointments, which can be found reflected in various of his poems. Without so many of these experiences he might have found writing easier, and written more fluently. They compensated him, on the other hand, with a kind of stoic fortitude, leavened by a wry humour. When he was asked to take over the editing of a drooping left-wing literary magazine for Eastern countries, he came to Edinburgh to see me, and we had long talks about what could be made of it—the obvious first need being to get rid of its absurd title, *Lotus*. He chose Beirut as a base, but it proved to be a very unlucky one. I got some news in a long letter from his wife. She talked of living on a powder-keg, and of the nearby Iraqi Airlines office being bombed by a guerrilla group in the small hours,—'the building shook—and I shook for days—Faiz merely turned over and said "Go to sleep again".' But before long Beirut proved impossible.

The same letter reminds me that at that time Alys was thinking of collecting the memories of her life and its ups and downs, and that Faiz had promised a publisher to do the same. I never heard how far these projects got, but Alys had a sense of history of every kind, and of the bygone echoes and associations clinging to the past. She wrote a series of articles about survivals from the old Lahore, and how antique shrines and dwellings were mouldering away for want of anyone to take care of them. I had known her in England before either of us found ourselves in the East. Few women anywhere could have received so touching a tribute from their partner as the quatrain, no. 21 in this collection.

In another way, Faiz himself might be thought of as a protector and preserver of Urdu from the encroachments of English. Already a long time ago, in 1834, Thomas de Quincey was writing in his *Reminiscences of the Lake Poets*: 'The English language is travelling fast towards the fulfilment of its destiny...its ultimate mission of eating up, like Aaron's rod, all other languages.' Faiz welcomed translations of his work, which (in what is called 'free verse') have been plentiful. I was, I believe, the first to try, at his own invitation. But lately it has become a vogue in Pakistan to write poems, as well as stories, in English, instead of in any of the national languages. Faiz would not have approved of this.

'A part of me seems to have died with him', an Urdu novelist of Lahore, an old friend of ours, wrote to me with the news of Faiz's death in December 1984, at the age of 73. A little later I read of the large meeting called in Lahore to pay homage to his memory; a mixed gathering with many from the working classes, progressive students, and others, whose side he had taken all his life.

Stow, Selkirkshire
13 August 1999

V. G. KIERNAN

# CONTENTS

## POEMS FROM *PRISON THOUGHTS* (ZINDĀṄ-NĀMA) 1956



## POEMS FROM *DURESS* (DAST-E-TAH-E-SAṄG) 1965



## UNCOLLECTED POEMS

# FOREWORD

This volume is an expansion of a set of verse translations from Faiz which were begun in a forest rest-house on the banks of Woolar Lake in Kashmir in the summer of 1945, continued at intervals over the next dozen years, and published in 1958 at Delhi (later reprinted at Lahore). These translations have now been revised throughout, and also brought into line with the latest editions of the originals: Faiz is a reviser and polisher, as careful literary craftsmen have often been, and has made various alterations over the years. Sixteen poems are added, from his last published collection and from some recent verses that have not yet appeared in book form. All these, like most of the former set, were chosen by Faiz himself, and all the translations have been discussed with him.

In addition, this volume contains the Urdu text of each poem, with a romanized transliteration and a literal prose rendering. This apparatus is designed to assist Western students of the language, who are beginning to be rather less few than they used to be; it is hoped that it may be of service also to some East Pakistanis and Indians desirous of acquainting themselves with the Urdu literature of West Pakistan. Even to readers not concerned with the language it may be hoped that the Urdu text will make an artistic appeal. It has been written by Syed Saqlain Zaidi, reputed by many to be one of the finest copyists now working in Pakistan of the *nasta'līq* form of the Arabic script, which developed in Persia by the fifteenth century and went through a further evolution in Indo-Pakistan.

An experiment at turning this script into roman letters may not be without interest for Urdu-speakers familiar with English, besides its practical value for learners of Urdu. It must I think be admitted that while the Persian-Arabic script can be exquisitely ornamental, it is far less well adapted to the requirements of a utilitarian age. Even as calligraphy it is already, according to many connoisseurs in Pakistan, a declining art in which a *kātib* such as Syed Saqlain Zaidi is likely to have few successors. Like the Chinese characters, it grew in a society where writing was confined to a few; both, possibly, may have a better chance of keeping their artistic quality if their more modern and mundane duties are handed over to the workaday alphabet that has already been adopted in Turkey and debated in China and India. Faiz's poems, it may be remarked, are circulating in India not only in Urdu script but also in the less decorative but far more scientific Nagari script of Hindi, without losing much by the change except in the eyes of lovers of *nasta'līq* whose loyalty to it, aesthetic or sentimental, can only be respected.

I am grateful to the People's Publishing House of Delhi for readily acceding to the re-issue of the translations published by it; and to Mr Altaf Gauhar, a senior civil servant at Rawalpindi, for lending his good offices towards securing the approval of the Government of Pakistan for the preparation of this volume under the auspices of Unesco. I owe many thanks to Syed Saqlain Zaidi for the patience and skill with which he adapted himself to the exceptional demands made on him by the plan of this edition; also to Syed Babar Ali, once a pupil of mine in the Aitchison College at Lahore and now managing director of the firm of Packages Ltd there, for generously lending the services of this distinguished *kātib*, who has been in his firm's employment. With regard to the rest of the work, my own knowledge of the language and its literary complexities is very far from sufficient to have enabled me to get on without a great deal of aid and counsel. 'Truly, sir, in respect of a fine workman, I am but as you would say a cobbler.' In an undertaking beset with so many linguistic and technical problems I cannot hope in the end to have avoided all errors, and for whatever errors may remain I must blame myself and not my counsellors. Among these Vazir ul-Hasan Abedi, Reader in Persian at the Oriental College of the University of the Panjab at Lahore, has been very helpful on nice points both of text and of translation. Mr R. Russell, Reader in Urdu at the London School of Oriental Studies, gave me the benefit of his knowledge of systems of transliteration from Urdu; and he was kind enough to read and point out lapses in the first draft of the Introduction, as was also Faiz's and my old friend of Lahore days, Mr Som Nath Chib. Faiz himself, besides supplying many elucidations of meaning, and other information, likewise read this draft, and made a number of criticisms which I have been happy to avail myself of, even if I cannot feel sure that even now everything in it would meet with his agreement. His wife has been invaluable in expediting correspondence on all these matters.

I owe it to two others to say that without their help and encouragement, continued over a good many years, the work could not have been carried out at all. Sardar Malik Khayyam d'Ashkelon, of the Arts and Letters Division of Unesco at Paris, has been indefatigable in smoothing away the numerous obstacles that have cropped up, at the cost of having to write enough letters to fill another tome. With such representatives Unesco can worthily play its part as patron of letters, modern successor to Harun al-Rashid or Lorenzo the Magnificent. In thanking once again one of my oldest friends, Dr Nazir Ahmad, lately Principal of Government College, Lahore, I have to repeat what I have written elsewhere, that my translations from both Faiz and Iqbal would have been impossible without the benefit of his literary knowledge and judgment and his unlimited generosity in bestowing them, and his time and labour, on others. For the present edition he took on himself the further and onerous duty of preparing the Urdu text. But I should exhaust myself in what to anyone unacquainted with him would appear hyperbole, if I tried to do justice to the qualities for which Dr Nazir Ahmad is known in his own country to a host of admirers in every walk of life.

V. G. KIERNAN

# PREFACE

## 1. *Principles of Translation*

All translation of poetry is a horn-window, allowing only a certain quantity of light to pass through it; a proposition in support of which innumerable quotations might be assembled. On the special problems of translation from Urdu, and the principles I have tried to follow, I may refer the reader to the 'Note on the Translations' in my collection of poems from Iqbal, published in 1955 in the *Wisdom of the East* series. In general my aim has been to render as well as I could in English verse the poetical colouring of the original while deviating as little as possible from its sense. Comparison with the literal translations that accompany the verse ones in this volume will show how often some departure is unavoidable. But the precise sense or shade of meaning in some lines, especially of Faiz's later poems, may be differently felt by one reader or another, even among those brought up on the language. It might be supposed that reference to the author would clear up any uncertainty; but it is not always easy to get him to choose between two or three slightly different versions, not from any lack on his part of familiarity with nuances of English but, it would seem, because in his own mind too shades of meaning may waver or melt into one another. It may indeed be generally true that a poetic phrase or image has, like each word by itself, not a single meaning but a band of related meanings, and for its inventor as well as for his listeners.

When Laura Lafargue was translating some poems, she and Engels agreed that metre and rhyme ought to be faithfully reproduced. This would be a counsel of perfection impossible to follow in full. Urdu prosody rests on a basis too remote from that of English to be reproduced with any exactness; while rhyming is so much more facile than in English as to have a much less insistent effect, so that to copy it would often be undesirable, even if not impracticable. I have made some attempts to imitate metres of the original; and where my lines are of unequal metrical length, those of the original are so too. I have kept the rhyme-scheme of some poems in the *g͟hazal* form (AA BA CA DA . . .), where it has a special importance. Otherwise I have introduced rhyme in any quantity or pattern that seemed appropriate, or feasible.

In the 'Note' just referred to the reader will find some remarks on Urdu metres compared with Western; more systematic accounts of the former will be found in Duncan Forbes's *Grammar of the Persian Language* (London, 1876), and in Munibur Rahman's *Post-Revolution Persian Verse* (Aligarh, 1955). Attention may be drawn to a valuable essay by Ralph Russell, 'Some Problems of the Treatment of Urdu Metre' (*J.R.A.S.*, April 1960). This has the merit, among others, of raising the question of the part played by stress or ictus, which is clearly important in practice though it finds no place in Urdu metrical theory. This theory is, after all, a foreign one, imposed on a language that it only imperfectly fits; and the student soon comes on the awkward fact pointed out by Russell that in order to recognize the metre of a verse he must know how it is pronounced, but that—since there is an element of poetic licence here—in order to know how it is to be pronounced he may first need to know what metre it is in. Practising poets, Faiz among them, work by ear, not by formal rules, and are seldom able to explain to an enquirer what, in metrical terms, they are doing. In a line of Urdu verse spoken in ordinary tones a foreigner will not easily succeed in recognizing the rhythm; conversely, a born speaker of Urdu, however well-read in English, almost always finds English metre, blank verse above all, incomprehensible. We all, it is probable, hear the rhythm of verse far more with an inner ear, an invisible chronometer developed by long habit and familiarity, than with the ear of sense. The best advice that can be given to a novice is to hear Urdu verse recited in the emphatically rhythmic style common in public declamation.

Among some characteristic metres used by Faiz are the following, approximately expressed in the notation of our own classical verse with accents added to mark stress:

| – ⏑ –́ – | – ⏑ –́ – | – ⏑ –́ – | – ⏑ –́ |

(as in poem no. 1)

| –́ ⏑⏑ | –́ ⏑⏑ | –́ ⏑⏑ | –́ ⏑⏑ –́ |

(as in no. 9)

| ⏑ –́ – | ⏑ –́ – | ⏑ –́ – | ⏑ –́ – |

(as in no. 10)

| ⏑ – ⏑ –́ – | ⏑ – ⏑ –́ – | ⏑ – ⏑ –́ – | ⏑ – ⏑ –́ – |

(as in no. 18)

| ⏑ – – –́ | ⏑ – – –́ | ⏑ – – –́ | ⏑ –́ |

(as in no. 25)

| ⏑ – – –́ | ⏑ – – –́ | ⏑ – – –́ | ⏑ – – –́ |

(as in no. 26)

## 2. *The Urdu Text*

The Urdu text was prepared by Dr Nazir Ahmad, and the following remarks on problems and methods are based on explanations supplied by him.

A good many niceties of pronunciation can be indicated in the Arabic script only with the aid of diacritical signs. This applies of course particularly to vowel sounds, as there are letters for only three long vowels (two of which are also consonants) and none for short, except the *hamza* (ء). This is classed as a vowel, short *alif*, and can carry diacritical signs; but in most respects it might better be regarded as itself one of these signs, showing (like the ¨ or diaeresis in English) that a vowel sound is being followed by another and distinct one.

In the employment of the signs, usage may go to either of two extremes. Sometimes, in school primers, or in the writing of Koranic quotations, every letter is accompanied by a sign. Far oftener, in books and especially newspapers, only the barest minimum is employed. To follow the first of these procedures would have been to clog the text with an extravagant number of markings, and seriously detract from its calligraphic charm. To follow the second would have meant leaving the student without the guidance he will probably often need. A middle course has therefore been adopted. It owes something to the model of the Urdu schoolbooks prepared in the later nineteenth century under the guidance of an English Director of Education in the Panjab, Holroyd, where a restricted but methodical use was made of diacritical signs, with good results.

No new signs have been concocted (though one or two are really needed); all those in the text are in familiar use.

The *zabar*, or *faṭha* ( َ ), commonly indicates that a consonant is 'movent', i.e. is followed by the indeterminate vowel sound (of 'u' in English *cut, but*). It is omitted in this text wherever it can be taken for granted, as in syllables equivalent to English *cut*. It is always inserted, however, when its effect is to change the sound of the vowel *ye* from broad 'e' (as in *ret*, or English *rate*) to 'ai' (as in *jaise*, *khair*, or—roughly—English *hair*); or to change the sound of the vowel *vow* from 'o' (as in *bolnā*, or English *boat*) to 'au' (as in *haule*, *aur*, or—roughly—English *oar*).

The *zer*, or *kasra* ( ِ ), is always inserted in this text when it indicates, as it normally does, that a consonant is followed by a short 'i', or less often a short 'e' (as in English *him*, *hem*). It is inserted also when, under a consonant preceding the vowel *ye*, it gives this the vowel sound of English *feet* instead of *fate*; except that it is omitted when this vowel stands at the end of a word, since there are then two ways of writing it to distinguish the two sounds.

The similarly written *izāfat* sign, which placed under the last letter of a word links this grammatically with the next word (as in *Dast-e-ṣabā*), is never omitted in this text.

The *pesh*, or *ẓamma* ( ' ), which indicates that a consonant is followed by a short 'u' (as in English *pull*), or gives a following vowel *vow* the sound of long 'u' (as in English *rule*) instead of 'o' (as in English *rote*), is always inserted.

The *jazm* ( ^ ), indicating that a consonant is *sākin* or 'quiescent', i.e. not vowelized, is inserted except at the end of a word, where it is to be taken for granted. It is placed over a terminal *vow* to denote that this letter represents the consonant 'v' or 'w', instead of the vowel. Conversely, it has been put over the *vow* that often links a pair of nouns (e.g. *bāgh-o-bahār*) to make it clear that this 'and' is the Persian *o* and not, as it might be, the Arabic *wa*.

The *shadd* ( ᵚ ), which doubles the consonant under it, is always inserted.

The *madd* ( ~ ), which prolongs the sound of a letter in some Arabic words (normally in Urdu that of a long 'a'), is inserted in the few cases where it occurs.

Where the letter *nūn* has the sound of a nasal 'n', the dot is omitted from the form in which it is written at the end of a word; elsewhere it is marked by an inverted *jazm* ( ˇ ) above it.

When the consonantal *vow* ('v' or 'w') is silent, this is indicated by a dash under it ( _ ).

It will be observed that in this text *he* or 'h' is written in the 'two-eyed' form (*hā-e-makhlūṭa*) only when it aspirates a preceding consonant (as in *bhār*); and that it is uniformly written in two other ways according as it (1) is sounded separately but in writing is joined on to both the neighbouring letters (as in *bahār*), or (2) is not so joined to the preceding letter (as in *wahāṅ*): in this case a *shosha* ( ͺ ) is placed under it.

When vowel sounds are to be fully expressed in writing, it sometimes becomes necessary to choose between variant ways of pronouncing a word; and the pronunciation current among educated people may not be that favoured by most dictionaries. Thus the word for 'love' that all but a few purists pronounce as *muḥabbat* is given by the dictionaries its Arabic sound, *maḥabbat*, which has been adopted here.

### 3. *The Transliteration*

There is at present no generally accepted system of romanization for Urdu, and diverse experiments continue to be tried. Special problems are created by the mixed origins of the language. It has first to be decided whether a transliteration should be content to reproduce sounds (like the method approved in 1958 by the American Council of Learned Societies) or should discriminate between different letters with the same sound. Urdu has four letters all pronounced identically like the English 'z'. They may all be written as 'z'; but then etymology is lost, and, a more practical point, the student is given far less help in deciphering the Urdu script, a baffling one (being, in effect, a species of short-hand) for most readers not familiar with it from childhood, even when written, as in this volume, far more legibly than it usually is. Search for unfamiliar words in a dictionary is also rendered harder. I have, therefore, kept to the principle of each Urdu letter being given a specific counterpart in the romanized version.

There next arises the question of how to modify the roman letters so as to enable them to make these distinctions, and to express sounds not found in English. Each of the many languages employing roman script makes its own modifications; by means of accents, as in French, or by particular conventions (so that for instance 'ch' in French is sounded like 'sh' in English). As between these two methods, it seems to me better to employ additional signs or accents, than to attach arbitrary values to letters. All the four Urdu letters sounded as 'z' are here rendered by the letter 'z', with distinguishing signs added. The other method may be illustrated from the system worked out for a selection from Ghalib about to be published by the Muslim Progressive Group of Delhi: there, for example, 'c' represents 'ch' as in *church*. To me it appears that the further one goes in thus attaching novel values to letters, the more the benefit of a familiar script is lost, until at a certain point it would seem logical to go the whole hog and use the international phonetic symbols.

Use and wont have, over the years, led to a number of practices being commonly adopted. It seems desirable to retain most of these, and also to keep as close as possible to the standard transliteration of Arabic. My procedure is based on that of J. T. Platts's Dictionary of 1884, with some changes for the sake of simplicity or conformity with general usage. The consonants, in Urdu alphabetical order, are then as shown on the following page.

| | | | |
|---|---|---|---|
| *be* | b | *sīn* | s |
| *pe* | p | *shīn* | sh |
| *te* | t | *suād* | ṣ |
| *ṭe* | ṭ | *zuād* | ẓ |
| *se* | s̤ | *toe* | t̤ |
| *jīm* | j | *zoe* | z̤ |
| *che* | ch | *'ain* | ' |
| *ḥe* | ḥ | *ghain* | *gh* |
| *khe* | *kh* | *fe* | f |
| *dāl* | d | *qāf* | q |
| *ḍāl* | ḍ | *kāf* | k |
| *zāl* | z | *gāf* | g |
| *re* | r | *lām* | l |
| *ṛe* | ṛ | *mīm* | m |
| *ze* | z | *nūn* | n (when nasal, ṅ) |
| *zhe* | *zh* (the sound of 's' in pleasure) | *vow* | v or w (when silent, w) |
| | | *he* | h |
| | | *ye* | y |

There are no doubt possibilities of confusion in the use of 'h' following other consonants, and it must be pointed out that while in this scheme 'ch' and 'sh' have their English values, 'th' and 'ph' have not, but are 't' and 'p' aspirated, on a par with 'bh', 'kh', etc. They might have been written as 't'h', 'p'h', but this seemed unnecessarily cumbrous, except in one or two cases to indicate the omission of a short vowel normally present between the two letters (as in poem no. 34, line 12, *saṭ'ḥ* instead of *saṭaḥ*). When 's' and 'h' are, as occasionally, separate letters standing side by side, they are written 's'h'.

The short vowels expressed in the Urdu text by the signs explained above are rendered as 'a' (the indeterminate vowel), 'ĕ', 'i', 'u'. The long vowels are written as 'ā', 'e'. 'ī', 'ɔ', 'ū'.

In other words, 'a', 'i', 'u' when not otherwise marked are short; 'e' and 'o' when not otherwise marked are long. These last two being long in the great majority of cases, it seemed unnecessary to put an accent over them all the time.

*Vow* bearing a *zabar* sign is written as 'au', and *ye* with this sign as 'ai'.

Where two adjacent vowels are separate sounds instead of diphthongs, I have put an apostrophe between them (which thus serves a similar purpose to the *hamza*)—as in words like *ko'ī, hū'e, ā'ī*.

Words in Urdu verse are fairly often modified to meet metrical requirements. Consonants may be doubled, as in *likkhūṅ* for *likhūṅ* (no. 52, line 18), or *rakkhā* for *rakhā* (no. 6, line 5). Or a consonant may be omitted, as in *hāt* for *hāth*. A vowel may be shortened, e.g. *dukān* for *dūkān*, or *guhar* for *gauhar*. All these changes are represented in the Urdu text and reproduced in the transliteration; also suppressions of the indeterminate short 'a' vowel, as in *guzrā* for *guzarā*. In the opposite and more frequent case where terminal consonants are given this vowel for the sake of metre, when in prose they would not have it (as in French verse a silent terminal 'e' is sounded when the next word begins with a consonant) it is left to the reader, as he acquires a familiarity with the rhythm, to supply the unrecorded sound for himself.

A further necessary caution is that Urdu is not in all respects phonetic. Thus the word *maḥfil* sounds in ordinary speech like 'mĕḥfil', and *bahut* like 'bohat'; and since the letter *'ain* is silent but may lengthen a preceding vowel, a word such as *va'da* sounds like 'vāda'. The transliteration does not attempt to give the sound of such words as they are pronounced, but a transcript of how they are written. I have, however, felt that a few short words very frequently recurring ought to be written as nearly as possible as they sound. Hence *wuh* ('that') is written *vo*, and *yih* (this') as *ye*.

For the same reason I have occasionally used the sign ˘ to mark the vowel 'e' as short (as in English *hem*). Urdu script does not distinguish between this and short 'i', and the two sounds (partly perhaps because not usually marked in writing at all) run into each other. Yet in some very common words the sound is fairly distinctly that of a short 'e', and I have marked it so in particular in *mĕrā*, *tĕrā* ('my', 'your'), the metrically lightened forms of *merā*, *terā*, where the alternative, *mirā* or *tirā*, would be far from the actual sound. I have also written *pa(h)* ('on') phonetically as *pĕ*. But in general where this vowel sound occurs I have given the letter corresponding to the one in the Urdu word as written; e.g. *pahlā* ('first'), though the sound is in fact *pĕhlā*. I write 'e' for the *iẓāfat*, as more common now than the formerly preferred 'i', and closer to the sound (*Dast-e-ṣabā*, instead of *Dast-i-ṣabā*), but have not tried to define the quantity of the vowel, which may be anything from very light to very heavy according to its metrical position.

I have followed old practice in using hyphens to link the *iẓāfat* 'e' with both the neighbouring words, and also with any following words that its grammatical influence as a conjunction extends to, though this sometimes produces a rather long chain of hyphenations. An exception is a phrase like *shab-e sust mauj* (no. 19, line 6), where an adjective intervenes between the *iẓāfat* and the noun governed by it.

I have used hyphens also between pairs of words linked by *o* ('and'), but only when the two words are so closely associated by meaning or convention as to form really a single compound, e.g. in no. 23, line 34, *lauh-o-qalam*, but *ṯabl o 'alam*.

I have thought it helpful to put hyphens between some common prefixes and their nouns (*be-kas*, *be-tāb*, *nā-tawān*); and between one or two suffixes and their pronouns (*mujh-ko*, *jis-se*), though it may be noted that in modern Urdu writing the tendency is to write these as separate words instead of running them together as formerly.

Enclitics are joined to their nouns or pronouns with hyphens, e.g. *safaid-sā* ('whitish'), *chhanaktī-hī* (no. 15, line 16); *maiṅ-ne*, *ṣabā-ne*.

In the romanized text punctuation is supplied; in the Urdu text no more could be done, without disfiguring the calligraphy, than to make a few tentative insertions. The refined Western art of punctuation has no counterpart in the East; in Urdu verse it must have been discouraged both by the prevalence of the end-stopped line and couplet, and by the habit of listening to poetry rather than reading it. At its present stage of development Urdu would seem to an onlooker to stand in urgent need of a system of punctuation. In the meantime the student of Urdu verse must learn to appreciate the differences between its flow, its natural intervals, its logic of imagination, and those of Western poetry.

# INTRODUCTION

Poets in this century, like leaders of nations, have emerged from some unexpected nooks and corners. Faiz Ahmed's forbears were Muslim peasants of the Panjab, that green patch between mountain and desert, between middle India and inner Asia. His father, born with the instincts of a wanderer, set off in early life to Afghanistan, where he rose high in the service of the Amir 'Abd ul-Rahman,[1] and acquired some of the habits of a feudal grandee. Having fallen foul of his royal employer and escaped in disguise, he turned up in England, where his advent aroused curiosity in the highest circles: Afghanistan was always a sensitive spot in the perimeter of the empire. Cambridge and Lincoln's Inn, a bizarre exchange for Kabul and Kandahar, made a lawyer of him, and he returned at length to his birthplace to practise: not with great financial success, for lavish habits were hard to shake off, and an old man's tales of bygone splendour fell on less and less credulous ears.

If his son inherited an adventurous bent, his journeys of discovery were more of the mind, and it was not until long after he had grown up that he roamed far from home. It may have been a good thing for him that he did not go to Europe to study, as a young man of wealthier family would have done. Too many Indians of that day came back from the West full of enthusiasms that failed to survive transplantation, or that they could not spread to others. Faiz Ahmed imbibed the ideas of the nineteen-thirties, more gradually but tenaciously, from books or smuggled pamphlets, travellers' tales, and that impalpable genie known as the Spirit of the Age. They rooted themselves in his own soil, he saw them and their shadows by familiar sunlight; they took possession of his imagination, a stronghold from which ideas are less easily dislodged, as well as of his mind.

He studied, chiefly philosophy and English literature, at Lahore, the provincial capital and centre of the network of affiliated colleges making up the University of the Panjab, where a number of gifted young men came by education in the fullest sense of the word. In due course he gained a junior lecturing post in a college at Amritsar, where I first had the good fortune to get to know him, thirty years ago. It was a Muslim college in the city sacred to the Sikhs, where the communal passions already fermenting were strong. But there was no hostile frontier then as now between Amritsar and Lahore, and the Panjab was still in many ways a Sleepy Hollow where life moved at the pace of the feeble cab-horses drawing their two-wheeled *tongas*; where young men could indulge in old carefree idle ways, with long hours of debate in coffee-houses and moonlight picnics by the river Ravi. In this mode of living, verse-making played a part it has long since lost in the busy practical West. It was a polite accomplishment, a hobby cultivated by men, and a few women, in varied walks of life; often, to be sure, a racking of brains over elusive rhymes not much more elevating than a Londoner's crossword-puzzle. The *mushā'ira* or public recitation by a set of poets in turn, the novice first, the most admired writer last, was a popular social gathering, as it still remains; an audience would often guess a rhyme-word or phrase before it came, and join in like a chorus. Radio, then getting under way, was lending it a new medium, broadening into an entertainment for a whole province what had begun long ago as the recreation of a small Court circle. It might be highly artificial, as when participants were supplied beforehand with a rhyme to manipulate; and a scribbler well endowed with voice could make the most hackneyed phrase or threadbare sentiment sound portentous by delivering them in the half-singing or chanting (*tarannum*) fashion, or the declamatory style of recitation, that many affected. Still, the institution has helped to keep poetry before the public, and, along with floods of commonplace, to make known an occasional new talent.

Faiz Ahmed rhymed with the rest, and unlike some innovators complied with usage by adopting a pen-name or *takhallus*—that of *Faiz*, meaning 'bounty' or 'liberality':[2] looking back one may be tempted to read into it a meaning not yet in his mind, dedication to the service of his fellow-men. He emerged quickly from among the poetasters of whom every year engendered a fresh swarm, though not by dint of cultivating an aesthetic deportment, as some did. To outward appearance he was a good-natured, easy-going fellow, fond of cricket and dawdling, those favourite pastimes of Lahore, and readier to let others talk than to talk himself. It was characteristic of him that when reciting his verses, whether among a few friends or in a crowded college gathering, he spoke them quietly and unexcitedly.

Their quality was naturally mixed. The fine quatrain that stands at the beginning of his first book of verse published in 1941 (no. 1 in this anthology) was not the first to be written. He began with exercises, conventional enough, on well-worn topics, sighing over the cruelty of a non-existent mistress or extolling the charms of the grape. These also were invested with some fanciful attributes, for beer and whisky, not wine, were the liquors that the British presence had familiarized in India, and for literary purposes a beverage had to be poured not from bottle into glass but from flask into goblet. (*Shīsha*, a classical word, has come to be used for 'tumbler', but there is no term for 'bottle' except the impossible English word, spoken with a long 'o' and rhyming with Indian pronunciation of 'hotel'.)

But if Lahore was still on the surface an uneventful place, the tides of history were washing to and fro in India and the world outside, and their ripples reaching the Mall Road and the Kashmir Gate. Independence was only a decade away, and Faiz's lines were soon being coloured by patriotic feeling: almost as soon, by socialist feeling, for socialism was the new revelation that young idealists could invoke to exorcise communal rancours, by uniting the majority from all communities in a struggle against their common poverty, and to make independence a blessing to the poor as well as to the élite. History was to take a different turning; older forces and allegiances were to prove stronger, for a long time to come at least. But for young poets and story-writers national and social emancipation seemed to go together, and both to go with their own new-found freedom to try new subjects and methods. They were reading, and sometimes imitating (Faiz seldom if ever did this directly) Western writers like T. S. Eliot and Auden and Day Lewis. Their Progressive Writers' Association was a force in the land, and the Panjab had its own branch. Besides taking part in this Faiz, with the realistic sense he has always had that the poet is also a citizen, was getting in touch with groups of workingmen, and would spend evenings teaching them reading and writing and the ABC of politics.

Indian marriages were not made in heaven, but arranged, as they still often are, by careful parents, particularly in respectable Muslim families, whose women went out heavily veiled from head to foot. Faiz was once comically indignant at being invited to speak on Shakespeare in a girls' college, and made to address an unseen audience from the other side of a screen. In such an environment there was a double blessing for him in his marriage with an Englishwoman of remarkable character (whom I have the good fortune to have known even longer than I have known him); she has been ever since his best friend and guardian angel, and, with two daughters he is devoted to, has brought into his life a security that nothing else could have given it.

Before 1939 he had made a name for himself in literature; the war and its aftermath made room for him in political history too. This is not the place for a detailed review of his political or civic activities, but it is proper to emphasize that the ideals inspiring them have had a vital part in his literary development as well. They involved him in dilemmas inescapable in an India verging on revolution or civil war, and then in a raw new Pakistan painfully collecting itself into a nation. No straight road through this chaos was to be found, and every individual had to make decisions of his own. In all that part of the world movements and loyalties have been apt, like its rivers, to come and go suddenly, one day in full spate, the next dried up. Faiz has remained all this time faithful to what might be called an enlightened, humanistic socialism; the kind of activity open to him has fluctuated with circumstances.

After the Nazi invasion of the Soviet Union in 1941, Faiz like many Indians saw the war in a new light, as a contest in which the destinies of mankind were at stake, and with the approval of his associates joined the welfare department of the army; he was to be met with now on the Mall in the uniform of a lieutenant-colonel, solemnly returning salutes from British soldiers. After independence came in 1947, accompanied by partition, he continued to hope, as he has always done, for good relations between the two countries. When Gandhi was murdered by a Hindu fanatic, for trying to protect the Muslim minority in India, Faiz was, as a London newspaper said, 'a brave enough man to fly from Lahore for Gandhi's funeral at the height of Indo-Pakistan hatred'.[3] This hatred had been inflamed by the massacres, most terrible in the Panjab, that raged during the process of partition. To Faiz these horrors could only be expunged by the building of his new nation on principles of social justice and progress. One of his best-known poems (no. 19 here) expressed the tragic disillusionment of finding the promised land a Canaan—or so it seemed to him—only flowing with milk and honey for feudal landowners and self-seeking politicians.

With the removal by death of Pakistan's first and most trusted leaders, and reform and development sluggish, this disillusion soon became widespread. Editor now of the *Pakistan Times* of Lahore, Faiz made use of prose as well as verse to denounce obstruction at home and to champion progressive causes abroad; he made his paper one whose opinions were known and quoted far and wide, with respect if not everywhere with approval. He served as vice-president of the Trade Union Congress, and secretary of the Pakistan Peace Committee. This period ended abruptly with his arrest, along with a number of other figures, civil and military, in March 1951. The Rawalpindi Conspiracy trial unfolded its slow and somewhat mysterious length, during which a death-sentence was a lingering possibility, down to 1953, when Faiz was condemned to four years' imprisonment.[4]

His health suffered, but he was able to read, and think his own thoughts, and collect materials for a long-promised (but still, alas, unperformed) history of Urdu literature. To him as a poet his prison term might be called a well-disguised blessing. His wartime work had been heavy; he lamented that as soon as a new couplet began to stir in his mind he had to get up and go back to his office. After the war his editorial desk was even more enslaving. He might indeed point to the files of his newspaper, as Lamb did to the ledgers of the East India Company, as his real works. Worst of all has been a social environment prodigally wasteful, everywhere south of the Himalayas, of the time of men whose time is of any value. Far more than in the West a writer's admirers show their appreciation of him by thronging about him and making it impossible for him to write, or to keep to any rational plan of work; custom imposes on all alike the same monstrous proportion of talking to thinking as that of sack to bread in Falstaff's tavern bills. Even Faiz's wife has only been able to rescue him by half or quarter from this asphyxiation. Prison enabled him to write what for him was a considerable number of poems, in which his ideals took on fresh strength by being alloyed with harsh experience, and which were eagerly devoured by the public, in spite of the charges weighing over him.

Released in 1955, Faiz took up journalism again, but this quickly brought another, briefer spell in jail, one incident in a prevailing confusion that political affairs were falling into, and that led to the assumption of power by the army.[5] This did away with political confusion for the next decade, but also with nearly all political life, and it drastically curtailed the freedom of the press. Faiz's health moreover was no longer good, and a habit of perpetual cigarette-smoking, with a marked prejudice against physical exercise in any form, has not in these latter years improved it. He had to look for other kinds of work, cultural rather than political and in a way more congenial. He helped to make a film, which won international awards, about the lives of the fisherfolk, whom he visited and greatly liked, among the rivers of East Pakistan. He had plans for a national theatre, and with his wife sponsored a variety of local dramatic experiments. Drama is an art that found no entry into Islamic countries through the ages, and that Faiz believed might have a serious function in a new nation like Pakistan. In other elements of culture Indian Islam was rich, and it was his design to bring to light all that was capable of healthy growth among them, to help to form them into a modern national culture. He went back to his first vocation, teaching, and undertook the reorganization of a Karachi college founded by charitable endowment for poor students. When politics began to throw off, early in 1969, a long immobility, his concern for the country's future showed itself as keen as ever. On March 1st he made a long statement, full of practical good sense, to a round-table conference of progressive groups at Rawalpindi.

He has been living of late years at Karachi, that odd medley of Victorian façades and modern industry and spreading suburban villas; always with a hankering for the picturesque dilapidation of the old city of Lahore, and even, in sentimental moments, for his paternal village, where it may be conjectured that he would quickly die of boredom. In these years he has travelled the world a good deal, as his literary fame spread; it was of course in socialist countries that he came to be known first. He has been in China and Sinkiang, and several times in the USSR, where a translation of all his poems in Russian verse was published in 1960; the Muslim areas of Soviet Asia had a special attraction for him, and he for them. He has been in the USA, and Cuba; and in England, though regrettably seldom, considering his English wife and friends and literary connections. Once he was tempted as far north as Edinburgh, where he found that he had miscalculated the temperature of a Scottish winter. Most remarkably, he has made frequent short visits to India. Urdu poetry has been one of the slender bridges left standing between the divided countries, and Faiz's poems are welcomed on both sides of the border. Some of his best poems have been in honour of peace.

Amid these gropings and wanderings Faiz has continued to write the short poems that made him famous. He has written, altogether, too little; a small collection of poems now and then, with gaps of years in between, and a number of essays, collected in 1964 into a volume of literary criticism. Not seldom his talent has been thought to be drying up, though it has always flowed again; not seldom he himself talks of giving up composition, which with him is not facile improvisation but demands long, arduous effort. It may be a related fact that any sort of communication with other minds has become for him, as he once said to me, more and more difficult. Through verse, when he is successful with it, he overcomes this difficulty; at a more modest level an evening's conviviality may transform him from a rather tongue-tied companion (a day with whom once reminded an intelligent young woman, a family friend of ours,[6] of the silences of Colonel Bramble) into a ready and entertaining talker, with a lively sense of humour that finds little or no outlet in his verses.

What he has written, however much less than what he might, has brought him to something like the position of an unofficial poet laureate in West Pakistan, a land where poetry still makes an appeal potent enough to disarm some political and even religious prejudice. Criticism, even abuse, for his opinions have never ceased to come his way, and there are traces of this to be discerned in some of his poems. To be a nationalist writer is easy, to be a national writer hard. As a poet whom his countrymen are proud of, and at the same time a target of frequent attacks, Faiz's situation has been a contradictory one, reflecting the contradictory moods of a nation still—as Iqbal said of all the East—in search of its soul.

Some of Faiz's poetry is simple and direct, but often it is couched in a literary idiom some knowledge of which is needed for its appreciation, and one more artificial—or artful—than most. Urdu itself as a language might be called a bundle of anomalies, beginning with the fact that this language of many virtues has no true homeland. It originated, from the early stages of the 'Muslim', or rather Central-Asian, conquest of India, as the lingua franca of the 'camp' (its name derives from the same Turki root as the English word *horde*). It was a mixture of the Arabicized Persian used by the invaders, themselves a miscellany of Turks and others, with some of the still unformed Hindi dialects of the upper Gangetic valley, or 'Hindostan'. In verb structure it was native Indian, a fact which entitles it to be classed as an *Indian* language; in vocabulary largely foreign, much as a simplified Anglo-Saxon base was overlaid after the Norman conquest with French or low-Latin words. Urdu and English both began, therefore, about the same time, as pidgin dialects, or hybrids, and gradually evolved into self-sufficient languages, with special qualities derived from their mixed antecedents, qualities of contrast and modulation of great significance for poetry. Some of Shakespeare's effects could only have been achieved in such a medium, and Urdu can combine the harmony of Persian with the energy of Arabic and the simplicity of rustic Hindi.

During its centuries of growth, Persian served as the administrative and literary language of the Muslim ruling circles, Sanskrit continued to be the learned language of Hindus. But Indian vernaculars, including Hindi, hitherto a group of dialects rather than a language, were also taking shape; and when with the crumbling of Muslim political ascendancy in the 18th century Urdu emerged as successor to Persian, it was bound to have to compete, sooner or later, with some of these others, Hindi in particular. Its original function as a lingua franca now belonged to the colloquial mixture often called 'Hindostani', on the level at which modern Urdu and Hindi are virtually identical. Muslims and Hindus had lived side by side for ages (and most Muslims were descendants of Hindu converts), and in humdrum practical matters understood one another well enough. For more complex ideas—which neither had in fact been cultivating with much freshness for a long time—they had acquired little of a shared vocabulary. Hence when modern conditions brought the necessity of thinking on new lines, an élite culture suffused on each side with religious influences drew them in opposite directions. Learned Urdu has a diction heavily Persian and Arabic, learned Hindi heavily Sanskritic; and their scripts, the Persianized form of Arabic on the one hand, the Nagari or Sanskrit on the other, complete their mutual unintelligibility. It would be like this in English if half its users formed their technical and philosophical terms from Hebrew instead of Greek, and used Hebrew letters instead of Roman. Thus Urdu, originally a channel between older and newer inhabitants of India, in the past century has come to be one of the stumbling-blocks to fellow-feeling.

Urdu had grown not where there were most Muslims, in modern West and East Pakistan, but where Muslim political and cultural ascendency was firmest, which was always in and round the capital cities—Delhi, Agra, Lucknow, Hyderabad. Muslim civilization everywhere in history has been an urban civilization. This means that today Urdu as a mother-tongue finds itself marooned in the heart of Hindu India, chiefly in the U.P., the old Hindostan, where some nationalists are disposed to question its title to exist, and some of its lovers—not all of them Muslims—regretfully feel it to be doomed to a slow decline; though on the other hand some new opportunities have come its way, notably in the cinema. In Pakistan it is being brought forward as a national language, as Hindi is in India. But East Pakistan has proved faithful to the Bengali that it shares with West Bengal in India. In the western Panjab, nucleus of West Pakistan, Urdu is the vehicle of literature, of the newspaper press, and of formal or ceremonial speech: it is employed for everyday purposes of writing, and is challenging English as the medium of higher education. But all familiar converse is carried on in Panjabi, a vernacular shared like Bengali with a province of India; a language, or as some would say a group of dialects, standing to Urdu in something like the relationship of the broadest of rural Scots to the most refined of Oxford English.

When the Mogul empire faded, and with it the old cultural links with Persia, it was chiefly the poetical part of the legacy of Persian that Urdu fell heir to. For public business, legal or administrative, and higher education, English was the successor. The Muslim community, socially an unbalanced one of feudal cast, with only an embryonic middle class, had few professional or commercial men with reason to write prose; and fallen from power, unable for long to adapt itself to new times, it had stronger feelings than thoughts, an impulsion towards emotional verse more than towards rational prose. In Ghalib the language found the poet still regarded as its greatest. He belonged, until the Mutiny swept it away, to the shadowy Mogul court at Delhi, with its poignant contrast between present and past to kindle his imagination. Urdu prose on the contrary was virtually making its first start with Sir Sayyed Ahmad,[7] who likewise began in Delhi but shook its ancient dust off his feet and entered English service before the Mutiny; his mental life was one of wrestling with the problem, for Muslim India, of its present and its future. Subsequent progress has been uneven, and since the birth of Pakistan it has been a disputed issue there whether, or how rapidly, Urdu can be made the medium of higher education, scientific included.[8] Faiz is one of those most firmly convinced that it is capable of meeting every modern requirement.

As a poetical medium, Urdu might almost be a language made up by poets for their own benefit; a one-sided benefit no doubt by comparison with Western languages like English whose foremost poets, from Shakespeare down, have so often been first-rate prose writers as well. But this double faculty may be a thing of the past. Modern English may be too far secularized, overloaded with utilitarian burdens, to be capable any longer of poetry. A language like Urdu, with a smaller prose content, has so to speak a lower boiling-point, and boils up into poetry—or vaporizes into verse—more readily. As one consequence of this freedom from dull workaday business, Urdu may have gone on being tied more closely than need be to the apron-strings of classical Persian. This continued to be studied and read after its fall from power in India, and in West Pakistan still is so quite widely. Almost any Persian noun or adjective might be brought into an Urdu verse, just as any Greek word can nowadays be incorporated into English prose. Persian syntax too, notably the use of the *iẓāfat* (-e-) to join a noun either with its adjective or with its possessive, is retained to a much greater extent than in prose. Until a generation ago a whole Persian line or couplet might be inserted in an Urdu poem.

Between Mutiny and Great War two shifts, not unrelated, were taking place in Urdu poetry. It was coming to be less a lament for a lost past, and more an expression of the sensations of a Muslim community struggling to find its place in a changed world. Secondly, its main inspiration was migrating, with the coming of Iqbal, from the old centres, Delhi and Lucknow, northward to the Panjab; from early in this century to the partition, the two regions disputed the palm warmly between themselves, the older one priding itself at least on higher polish and technical proficiency. Some analogy may be drawn between them and their counterparts in Ireland. In Hindostan the leading Muslims were gentry of old family, descendants of conquerors from abroad, but becoming in course of time more 'Indian' than the solid mass of Muslims in the north-west; as the Anglo-Irish gentry in southern Ireland were in most ways except religion more Irish than the solid mass of Protestant settlers in Ulster. In Ireland's literary renaissance early in this century Anglo-Irish southern Protestants played a large part. Urdu poets in Hindostan had been playing some such part. The shift northward to the Panjab (which scarcely had a parallel in Ireland) meant in the long run a turning away from India, and presaged the birth of Pakistan—or so we may see it in retrospect—decades before anyone dreamed of such a thing.

On the surface the Panjab might have seemed too dull and torpid to be a nesting-place for poetry. There were only two big towns, and hardly any modern industry; big landlords loyal to the British power, the creator of many of them, held a preponderant influence. Geography has in some epochs isolated the land of the Five Rivers, at other times filled it with vibrations from round about, according to the condition in which neighbouring regions have been. When these have flourished, it has been a meeting-ground of ideas, as of trade-routes, instead of a backwater. It merges south-westward into the Indus valley, south-eastward into the Gangetic; north-east it has had historic links with Kashmir, north-west still closer ones with the frontier, Afghanistan, the roads into Persia and middle Asia. Hardly any other corner of Asia occupies such a focal position. Seldom since early Indo-Aryan times an intellectual leader, it has repeatedly been plunged by forces within and pressures from without into emotional and social turmoil. The coming of Islam, which in the end was to split the province in two, affected all of it in some degree, and helped to generate the ferment out of which came Sikhism, the one new religion that India with all its religiousness has given birth to since Buddhism. But this turned into a military domination, without much cultural vitality of its own; and in the 19th century Persia and central Asia, the old neighbours to the north, seemed to be at long last expiring, while British rule concentrated Indian energies in the seaboard provinces, and treated the Panjab mainly as a recruiting-ground for the army.

By the end of the century, however, Persia was rousing itself again, and Islam in Asia stirring in its sleep; while from southward the European ideas that had long been at home in Bombay and Calcutta were now filtering into the Panjab. As in other ages, these new currents were to make for bigger upheavals here than elsewhere, among a folk even in their physical proportions larger than life compared with most other Indians. Inevitably old communal jealousies would revive alongside of new things. Altogether it was a land riddled to an exceptional degree with contradictions old and new; one of sturdy peasants as well as landlords, one steeped in rustic humour and realism as well as possessing in Lahore a city which did not forget that it was once the Mogul imperial capital; a province that others seemed to have left far behind, but with lurking energies and untested capabilities waiting to break out, for good or evil, when the sleeping giant should awaken. It might even be said that Urdu poetry was taking wing to the Panjab because here it found most contraries and complexities to stimulate it. All three communities were writing Urdu verse, and in the same idiom; Muslims were easily in the lead, and have provided all the important names. Less at home in the new age than their Hindu neighbours they struck the visitor as having, by and large, less practical capacity, with far more imagination.

Tagore could address his Bengali compatriots in their own language, which besides a very long poetic tradition had also during the 19th century acquired a modern prose. Panjabi was rich in little but folk-poetry, and the chief other purpose it had served was as a vehicle for part of the Sikh scriptures, which invested it as a written language with associations distasteful to Muslims. They relegated it to colloquial purposes for which Urdu was too high-flown—somewhat as Beatrice told Don Pedro he was too fine a husband for her, she would need another for weekdays. For Urdu this was bound to involve a certain removal from actuality, such as Burns's verse underwent when he wrote in English instead of Scots. It brought the countervailing gift of an exotic, romantic vocabulary like a southern breeze laden with tropical scents. Words from far away make a more sensuously thrilling impression on the ear than familiar homespun ones, and through the ear on the fancy. Muslim habits of hearing or reciting Koranic passages in half-understood Arabic must have worked in the same manner. It may be guessed that the Urdu poet does not always have before his mind's eye so lively an image of the things he is speaking of as a European would; his mind is astir with words which are for him sounds, evocations, ancestral memories, less closely tied to tangible objects; of the 'two worlds' he so often sets against each other it is the invisible rather than the visible in which he is roaming.

All this harmonized with the situation of the Muslim class literate enough to have a full command of Urdu—though its poetical appeal could be felt more widely. It was a narrow middle class oriented by circumstances more towards fantasy than towards reality, overshadowed economically by Hindu competitors with far more capital, and also far more willingness to scorn delights and live laborious days in the pursuit of money. It was chronically pulled opposite ways: it wanted to grow, learn, move with the times—or, impatiently, leave them behind; both from diffidence about its ability to compete, and an inborn distaste for competitive moneygrubbing, it was often apt to shrink into its shell, to retreat along the old caravan trail winding away into the heart of Asia and its luxurious dream-world of shining dome and legend and remote superb names. Ultimately the outcome of these contrary impulses, irreconcilable within Indian horizons, would be the demand for a separate State. In the meantime Urdu and Urdu poetry were, next to religion, the Muslims' lifeline, giving them a sense of identity, a collective vision.

So much of the spirit and tone of Urdu poetry derives from Persian tradition that this ancestry must often be kept in mind, even when a poet like Faiz is alluding to quite contemporary matters. Verse forms and metres, besides diction, have helped to preserve continuity; and, still more strikingly, a common stock of imagery, which can be varied and recomposed inexhaustibly in much the same way that Indian (and Pakistani) classical music is founded on a set of standard note-combinations (*rāgas*) on which the performer improvises variations. All this was part of a culture that, like Europe's later, came into India fully-fledged, acquiring there a fresh colouring, new accompaniments—such as the *mushā'ira*—, yet never becoming altogether Indian.

Persian poetic attitudes were social. Whereas the Chinese poet so often purports to be wandering lonely as a cloud over his mountain, the Persian is to be found reciting in a 'circle', or 'gathering', or 'assembly', or breaking away from it only in a fit of literary frenzy. Behind this fiction lay the reception-room or hall of royal court or feudal mansion, where men of letters competed for the patron's favour and rewards; a rivalry of which today's *mushā'ira* is an imitation. Its setting was nocturnal, lamplit; a reader may call up in his mind the scene that Faiz evokes in a line of poem no. 23, a Mogul chamber with walls honeycombed into small niches, each holding its lighted candle. By time-honoured custom another candle or lamp was placed before each poet in turn as he recited. When we are transported out of doors it is to a garden, the formal garden or rather park with its water-channels running in straight lines from pool to fountain between flowerbeds and avenues, still to be seen in its perfection at Lahore in the Shalimar garden and the precincts of

Jahangir's mausoleum, or at Agra in those of the Taj Mahal: an exquisite oasis in a thirsty land, a paradise shut off from the sorry scheme of things outside by a rectangle of high wall. Here is the Islamic urban civilization refined to the last degree, a haven within a haven. On the scorched plains of upper India, as in inner Asia, Nature itself is man-made, the marble cascade replaces the waterfall, all the vulgar reality of yokel, spade, manure-heap is forgotten. Readers brought up on English poetry have found it easy to enter into the spirit of Chinese poetry, simple and naturalistic, haunted by the sound of rock-perched trees and winds; no poet from the Islamic realm has captivated them so much, except Omar Khayyam, self-banished into the wilderness that came up as close to the gates of the old cities of middle Asia as night in those latitudes succeeds day.

Faiz observed, when asked about this absence of free Nature, that the poets of former days were courtiers, feudal retainers of uncertain rank, whose duty was to be at hand whenever their patron wanted to be refreshed with wit or fancy, not to disport themselves in the countryside. He himself has a love of gardens, fostered by early acquaintance with the classic shades of Lahore, and with a later, less formal park there, the Lawrence (now Jinnah) Bāgh, one of his youthful haunts, for which he has pined during his sojourn in Karachi.[9] He is no gardener, but in jail did make an attempt at growing flowers from packets of seed requisitioned from distant Scotland, while a fellow-prisoner of more mundane tastes devoted his garden plot to rearing chickens.

Feudal patronage was capricious, and the rhymer often, like Shakespeare, in disgrace with fortune and men's eyes. It went with this, and with things deeper in the fibre of Indo-Muslim society, that though habitually addressing a company, he did so as an individual alone in the group: he assumed frequently a tone of repining, lamenting a hard lot in a bad world, the demeanour of a martyr, despised and rejected by men and mistress. This posture too has descended on much Urdu poetry of our time, producing on occasion a disparity almost ludicrous between a writer's heartbroken accents and his jolly countenance off duty. But the poet composing under the eye of an autocratic patron and of an inflexible religion could not give vent to his gloomier feelings in any open manner, or seem to be finding fault with the order of things as by God and the Sultan established. True, in the fiction of these symposia the patron was not supposed to be present in his own person: art requires some, if only fictitious, equality among its devotees, and the patron might be a poetaster himself, and take his turn to recite his own productions under his own pen-name. The last Mogul emperor, who had few cares of State to oppress him, was no mean performer. It was, then, the 'Saqi' who was supposed to preside, and be the centre of attraction: the wine-pourer, elevated into a mysteriously fascinating woman with whom all present were supposed to be hopelessly in love—an idealized, rarified version of the educated courtesan whose reception-room was the nearest that Muslim India could come to a European salon. It was under colour of bewailing the hard-heartedness of this demi-goddess that the poet could most easily give voice to his grievances against life at large. A true poet would be expressing something deeper than his own private disappointments. Ghalib we may think of as lamenting, in effect, the passing of an empire and a civilization, and generations of Muslim readers must have felt their own nostalgia echoed in his lines.

The oblique allusion, the conventional symbol, could be understood by each hearer in his own fashion, and applied to his own condition; for in that society all, from highest to lowest, were haunted by the same sense of mutability and insecurity, of the need for a protector. Hence evolved a kind of 'metaphysical' style, an elaborate play of fancy and ingenuity; once established, within a pattern of society only very sluggishly changing, this could keep a remarkably tenacious hold. It has kept it even in our changing times: abstracted and generalized in this manner, the perplexities and distresses of man's social being have from age to age a common complexion.

Love might stand for defiance, self-assertion, as well as resigned self-pity. It has played this part in many times and places, under a multitude of guises, always somewhere between life and art; where women went veiled it was bound to stand closer to art and fancy. The poet's world is an imaginary city, like that of Faiz's poem no. 47; Islam had no nations, any more than it had, culturally speaking, villages: as in old Italy a man's native town was his *patria*. In this city there is always a *Kū-e-malāmat*, or 'Street of Reproach': again a poetical depiction of the entertainers' quarter where courtesans and ordinary prostitutes and dancing-girls lived. Here a reckless lover will be carrying on a clandestine affair, heedless of the frowns of dull elders or precisians, the *rumores senum severiorum*. Or he may rush out from the town into the wilderness, and roam to and fro endeavouring to cool his distemper in its blank emptiness.[10]

All this lover's fever might represent, or the hearer was free to think of it as representing, the spiritual seeker's thirst for divine truth; and in this signification in turn, literal melted into metaphorical, and God himself might be either reality or symbol. In a society saturated with religious forms and phrases (though, like aristocratic Europe, seldom religious in its conduct) poetic imagery was bound to flow very often into their mould. In Islamic orthodoxy, there was small room for anything artistic, except the sublime simplicity of its best architecture. But side by side with it was the mystical cult of the Sufis, who sought through prayer and spiritual exercises, sometimes music and dance—eschewed by the orthodox—, even by means of drugs, to soar from the dull earth into contact with, or absorption into, the divine essence.[11] This cult came from Persia, but helped to make Islam in India more Indian, by its affinity with the *bhakti* stream in Hinduism. In the Panjab more than elsewhere the two escaped from the cloister and joined and fermented among common people, helping to create a body of folk-poetry where the religious brotherhood of man blended with thoughts of social equality, deliverance from feudal bonds.[12] Much of the mood and phraseology of Sufism, its catalogue of the 'states and stages' (*ḥāl-o-maqām*) of the pilgrim soul, its vital relationship between the spiritual guide and his disciples, was taken over into poetry, and had a further existence there as part of the counterpoint of mask and symbol. When a poet did not picture himself seated in a court circle, it would often be the circle of disciples round their master that he conjured up. Nor were the two so far apart as might seem; mystics had often clothed their thoughts in verse, courtiers and even rulers might also be disciples; a divine Beloved could melt imperceptibly into an earthly one, an ideal feminine, an unattainable mistress who was also the wine-pourer at the never-ending feast, as uncertain, coy, and hard to please as Fortune, dispenser of life's never-ending deceptions.

Love and religion shared besides a common emblem in wine, another refinement of gross fact into ideal essence. If in the feudal courts liquor forbidden to the faithful ran freely, and a Ghalib might be a serious drinker, poetically wine stood for exaltation, inspiration, and the tavern was the abode of truly heart-felt spiritual experience as opposed to the formal creed of the mosque. Drunkenness and madness are near allied, and the later—*junūn*, 'rapture' in the literal sense of possession by a spirit (*jinn*)—retained some of the aura that surrounds it among primitive people; it might be either the passion of the worshipper of beauty throwing the world away for love or the ecstasy of the acolyte despising material success in his heavenly quest.

All this vogue of 'madness' was a recoil from the hard fixity of life, the rigid framework within which man as a social animal imprisons himself, the sordid egotism forced on men who, whether poets or politicians, could only rise at one another's expense. It gave relief to the vague craving that every society generates, if only in its younger or more idealistic members, for something better, higher, freer. Against the omnipotence of Church and State there could be no rebellion; but veiled protest was allowable, under the form of praise of the individual prepared to defy convention, which as a harmless safety-valve became itself a tolerated part of the convention. Wine, love, mystic flights, were all momentary refuges from the bondage of reality. They fostered some poetry, as well as much literary posturing and affectation; the time would come when a poet like Faiz, standing at a new point in history, would be able to give them a fresh meaning, as symbols of a revolutionary challenge to the social order instead of a merely token defiance of it or a withdrawal from it into fantasy.

Ambiguity belonged to the essence of this style; in its visionary landscape things melted into one another like dreams, and everything had a diversity of meanings, or rather, any precisely definable 'meaning' was lost in a diffused glow. A poet might really have mystic moods, or might really be in love—with a woman, or, as in Greece or Rome, with a man; but for his poetry, for his hearers, that was not the real point, any more than for us when we listen to a piece of music whose composer may have felt religious, or been in love.[13] The most characteristic verse form was the *ghazal*, a string of any number of couplets in any one metre, rhyming AA BA CA DA. . . .[14] These should not aim at any obvious logical sequence, but owe their coherence to the recurrent rhyme and to a stream of association eddying beneath the surface. Its standard topic is love, its tone one of graceful trifling, and in ordinary hands it is not much more than a metrical exercise; so much so that in modern Urdu it constitutes a poetic hemisphere by itself, and a writer may be classed either as a serious poet or, with a touch of disparagement, as a *ghazal*-writer. The form has nevertheless been used by the foremost poets for the weightiest purposes; and it too has helped to provide a rainbow bridge between the impressionism of the past and the realism of the present.

One who notably turned the *ghazal* to new purposes was Mohamed Iqbal (1873–1938), the greatest Urdu poet to arise since Ghalib.[15] Born like Faiz at Sialkot, close to the mountains and close to the religious and cultural frontier that now divides India from Pakistan, he was a Panjabi of the professional middle class who wrote English prose and Urdu and Persian verse; a Panjabi, that is, whose mental horizons were far more expansive than those of his own province, and who as a result in some ways soared above its realities, in other ways fell short of them. In Urdu he wrote chiefly short poems, lyrical, religious, or satirical; in classical Persian long didactic poems addressed to the whole of Muslim Asia. He went through an early phase of addiction to English models, including description of Nature, and at the same time of attachment to the ideal, of equally Western source, of a free Indian nation with Hindu and Muslim as fellow-citizens. He studied in England and Germany, and was impressed especially by Nietzsche. Later his antipathy to Western imperialism in India and Asia deepened, but there came also disenchantment with the Indian national movement. He found an alternative in the vision, conjured up out of the hopes and doubts of his community, the Muslim middle class of the Panjab, of a grand Islamic revival and renewal, in which all the Muslim peoples should arise from their slumber, at once firm in their ancient faith and strong in modern knowledge. The glorious daybreak he was looking forward to did not dawn; most of the Muslim peoples were not yet finding their way either back to a renewed faith or forward to a modern organization. Even to him it grew clear that Pan-Islamic hopes would not be realized soon, and he turned his attention more to the predicament of his own community, and came to be identified with the programme of a separate Muslim state. He is therefore, though he died a decade before the partition, venerated—often uncritically, as in all such cases—as the moral founder of Pakistan.

Religious enthusiasm led Iqbal regrettably far towards seeing everything as an antithesis between Eastern faith and Western reason, identified with Western materialism and imperialism. Nietzsche too encouraged him to uphold the instinctive against the rational, feeling against thought. It was an antithesis that reflected the historical contradiction of his whole position; the inspiration of Faiz's life has been the hope of overcoming it with the aid of a new synthesis, that of socialism, seen as the reconciler of old culture and modern science in a refashioned society. He too doubtless has found history caught in unexpected crosscurrents, and not always moving as he hoped to see it. And despite the vast distance separating the two men, the prophet and the humanist, Faiz stands recognizably in the same line of succession. Iqbal left no true inheritor either of his philosophy or of his manner. But Faiz, who appeared on the literary scene just when Iqbal was departing from it, is not only the most gifted poetically of those who have come after: he has had all his life the same fundamental sense that poetry ought to be the servant of a cause, a beacon to 'poor humanity's afflicted will', not a mere display of ornamental skill.

Between the two a curious medley of contrasts and resemblances can be noted. In point of diction they are not very far apart, though Faiz has written verse only in Urdu, being no more drawn to Persian as a medium than, at the other extreme, to Panjabi. At certain moments he has achieved a striking simplification of expression (as in no. 11, a landmark of its period); more often his pen is dipped as deep as Iqbal's in Persian and Arabic. Even while he, along with most of the Muslim progressive writers of his generation, adhered as Iqbal had done in youth to the ideal of a united India, he was repelled by the prospect held up by Gandhi of a united 'Hindostani' language, a nondescript neither Hindi nor Urdu. There were many different roads by which a Muslim might travel to Pakistan. All the same, a fondness for allusion to things Hindu, even religious, has not left him; and it is worth while to observe that whereas Iqbal's great model and master was Rumi, the Persian mystical poet of mediaeval Asia Minor, Faiz has looked up above all to Ghalib, the arch-poet of modern Muslim India.

In the colouring of their work there is the strongest contrast between Iqbal and Faiz. At his most natural Iqbal is ardent, impetuous, direct; Faiz more delicately suggestive, and even less easily translated. One paints a picture that seems bathed in sunlight, the other in moonlight. Iqbal's daylight, on the other hand, owes little to our diurnal sun. As Faiz once pointed out in a lecture in London, Iqbal employs surprisingly little imagery of his own, and shows only the scantiest awareness of the physical world about him, no recognition of Nature except in some early poems. To the Western reader, brought up on naturalism, Faiz's own external world may appear stylized enough, like the landscape of a Persian miniature. But his imagery has grown increasingly free and profuse, until some of his later poems almost seem to dissolve in it.

Of his human environment each was keenly aware, each in his own way a 'committed' poet. Both combined older modes, elegiac, romantic, introspective, with a fresh note of criticism of society, and desire to alter it. Because they were animated by faith in something fresh and great, some cause above themselves for which to enlist public support, both were able to make use of the symbols their readers knew by heart, but to lend them fresh significance. Some contemporaries of Faiz, more negative and individualistic in outlook, were inclined to abandon them, in favour of a more direct and 'modern' handling of their subjects. For the poet appealing to collective emotions the symbols could still prove their value, clothing in familiar garb ideas too new and raw to be transformed immediately into poetry; though both Iqbal and Faiz might resort to them more sparingly as time went on.

Both frequently call up the traditional company of listeners, Iqbal—whose public recitations were confined as a rule to religious or political gatherings—assuming at times the figure of the spiritual leader seated among his disciples: Faiz haunted, in spite of republicanism, by whispers of long-crumbled palace halls. Iqbal was fond of the standard image of moth and candle, though his moth might now be a labouring class foolishly bowing before the idols of the rich.[16] Faiz has been loyal to that of garden and rosebed, a rosebed now as likely as not to typify the masses, the poor, buffeted by the rude winds of tyranny. In these literary parks the flowers are always crimson, and their colour carries overtones of passion, suffering, wounds. A comparison would be worth making with the swain and shepherdess and pipe of Europe's pastoral convention. A closer one would be with the use of peacock, deer, red flower, to symbolize longing for the lover in the Panjab Hill paintings of the eighteenth century.[17] In poetry the Western reader may be in danger of visualizing symbols too literally, and may do well to make an effort to see them from an indistinct distance, as things transmuted into thoughts, half-way towards the condition of the fossil imagery that all languages are strewn with.

Iqbal moved towards a Love that was a disembodied force, that meant also idealism, or enthusiasm, or *élan vital*. Faiz began with the stereotype of the cruel beauty, but a stable marriage, and domestic life of more modern pattern than Iqbal's, carried him towards an image more human and companionable, though still only elusively suggested by comparison with Western love-poetry, and, like the ghostly Saqi, interchangeable with other things, not now divine, but Cause, or Country, or People. It has been noted that Faiz has far more than Iqbal of a sort of 'masochism' habitual in Urdu poetry, which seeks the pangs of love rather than its fulfilment.[18] Iqbal's pan-Islamic thinking brought to his mind memories of the Muslim as world-conqueror; Faiz was concerned with the Muslim of his own times, as an underdog, and in some manner was able to fuse sympathy for hard-pressed labourer or peasant with the traditional griefs of the lover. In a society long accustomed to frown on free choice both in love and in political allegiance, each of these represented risk and adventure; and in Faiz's prison poems especially, separation from a woman and from a movement, or homeland, merge into one another. A Western reader may feel that this variant of the old symbolism succeeds better in a short piece like no. 25 than when elaborated as in no. 29; though this may be found interesting as an illustration, and perhaps as a further warning against figures of speech being taken too concretely. In like fashion wine may stand now for political truth or insight instead of spiritual, madness for the enthusiast's self-sacrifice in a progressive cause. Amid this readjustment or reshuffling, readers the best qualified may disagree about precise shades of intended meaning, as happened with some lines in no. 19 when it came out; or they may discover esoteric messages not intended at all by the author, whose poems are sometimes meant to mean no more than they say. No. 49, for instance, is a pure lyric.

Iqbal and Faiz both looked abroad for ideas as well as at home. Their Panjab has for ages been receiving from outside, from Persian, Greek, Turk, Briton, and yet has remained itself. Iqbal was only going to one more source when he brought Nietzsche into the Panjab, and Faiz when he helped to introduce Marx. Iqbal wrote of the tribulations of the poor majestically, as if looking down on them from heaven; he preached revolt of downtrodden peoples, relief of downtrodden classes by wealthier men infused with Islamic fraternalism. Faiz belonged to a generation that examined poverty at close range, with its dirt and its sores, and he learned its problems in social, economic detail. Still, Iqbal too had known of Marx, and paid tribute to him in more than one poem, and Faiz on his side has written verses religious in complexion.[18] It was not unfitting that in 1968 he helped to design a documentary film about the life-work of Iqbal, even if this aroused some conservative criticism by its emphasis on the radical notes in the elder poet's writings. Iqbal was an Islamic thinker with a strong dash of what has been coming to be known as 'Islamic socialism'; Faiz might be called a socialist with a groundwork of Muslim culture and feeling. He is indeed one of those many 'cultural Muslims' in many lands today who think of themselves not as religious in a specific sense but as heirs to a long experiment in civilization, and to a great ethical tradition which always did homage to truth and justice and to the upright man prepared to uphold them at all hazards. Pakistan's chance of growing into a nation both truly modern and genuinely founded on an Islamic past will depend, it may appear at least to an observer outside, more on the contribution of such 'cultural Muslims' than on anything else.

Iqbal and Faiz both belong very deeply to the Panjab, and when Faiz goes abroad it does not take long for him to begin to wish himself back in his own country. But both needed a world-vision to sustain them, a hope wider than their native limits, those of a province richer hitherto in promise than in fulfilment. Iqbal after his early travels shut himself up most of the time in a small room whence his thoughts could range abroad unchecked, and draw nourishment from an Orient that he half saw, half imagined. Faiz has had for a second or spiritual home the socialist lands, the socialist world movement, the peace movement. Disappointments with progress abroad as well as at home were bound to befall both. And though both achieved fame in their own country early, each often had occasion to feel misunderstood or isolated. Significantly, more than one poem by each of them has the title 'Solitude', and one of those by Iqbal[19] and one by Faiz (no. 8) are among their very finest. Between these two the contrast also is revealing. Iqbal's is in Persian. He is alone in a universe that still contains a God, though a distant and silent one; Faiz's knows only human beings, and they too are distant and silent. Iqbal as in many short and some long poems pictures himself as a traveller voyaging across immensities of space; Faiz is shut up in a deserted banqueting-hall, and it is night.

It may be remarked that in all this realm of poetry *death* is a far less prominent theme than it has always been in Europe. Exile, separation, loneliness, take its place, in a society more closely knit, in spite of wealth and poverty, than any known to the morbidly individualistic Europe of Horace, or Shakespeare, or our own day; a society of which the literary group gathered round patron or Saqi was the microcosm. Not the disappearance from life, but the banishment of the member from the group, has had, here as in Chinese poetry, the deepest poignancy. In other poems Faiz calls up imaginary companions to converse with in solitude, even (in no. 40) a personified loneliness. Two late poems (nos. 52 and 53) are concerned with illness, but what is uppermost in them is still not the thought of death in itself, but that of separation. Illness, like prison, divides and isolates. Social bonds so close-knit have made for social inertia, but there may be discerned in them now the possibility of transition to a new social order, of socialist character, and with this a survival of many values, human and cultural, likely to wither in a long interval of competitive industrialism, as the common man's feeling for poetry has withered in the West.

What relation there should be between artists and public movements has been the most crucial art-problem of our century. In Iqbal's case it may be open to conjecture that the short poems where he was able to fuse intense personal feeling with public themes will outlive his long didactic works. Faiz too at his best, as in poem no. 19, has succeeded in fusing them. But he has been taxed with trying at times too deliberately to be progressive, and writing verse more political than poetical. Some of this criticism may have been captious, but the risk is a real one. Even in some poems of high quality may be felt a certain faltering at the close, when he seems to try to resolve his discords without quite finding the right key.

He has been saved from becoming merely, or too facilely, a political writer, like so many others, or as Iqbal was too frequently preacher more than poet, by a strong inner resistance, a matter of both temperament and conviction. All imaginative writers are conscious of divided minds, opposing intuitions, and Faiz more than most. Readers have noticed how often in his earlier and middle work his poems turn—like no. 12, or no. 23, originally entitled 'Two Voices'—on a kind of duality, as if he were struggling to reconcile two contradictory visions of life. He is himself an odd mixture, an Oriental mixture, one is tempted to say, of indolence and energy, an inclination to contemplate existence through a cloud of cigarette-smoke and a compulsion to act. To get him to answer a missive is as nearly vain as any human endeavour can be; the 'violent hatred of letter-writing' that Coleridge found in Wordsworth is at least as strong in Faiz. Yet the spirit of the age has drawn him along a path necessarily toilsome, at times perilous.

Artists everywhere in our age, and the age itself in a vaster, more chaotic way, have faced conflicting claims of old and new, present and future, each right in its way; of Utopia and possibility, emotion and reason, worker and intellectual, individual and society. Perhaps by now we have seen enough to conclude that the artist's true function is not to identify himself too closely with one demand or the other, but to mediate or hold the balance between them. And perhaps it is in this direction that instinct and experience have guided Faiz. Some of his fellow-writers, in India and Pakistan as elsewhere, have withdrawn into ivory towers, some have made themselves mouthpieces of political leaders, some have stopped writing. Faiz's inner divisions, painful as they may have been, were a symptom rather of health than of weakness, of civic spirit combined with an artistic sense too strong to let him be swamped by the tidal force of a movement. Like all great and heroic movements the revolution of the twentieth century has been apt, to its own cost as well as theirs, to reduce individual men and women to units in its army, ciphers in its great account. The individual is nothing, the cause everything, proclaimed the Jacobins of 1793, and all world-overturners since then have echoed them. Accident has helped to save Faiz from being submerged; the absence in his own country of any strong organization with aims akin to his, which has thrown him most of the time on his own resources.

Two other magnets, literary conservatism and innovation, have exerted their rival pulls on him. His style has been altering in recent years, and becoming in some features more experimental. He has resorted fairly frequently, as he never did in earlier days, to what in Urdu is called 'free verse', which means not prose chopped up into odd lengths, as in English, but lines of varying length in one regular metre, an escape from the end-stopped couplet that has so often shackled invention. This more open manner has been accompanied by a wider choice of subjects, and a more flexible imagery. In other ways—whether or not belief in a planned pattern of society is related to respect for organized patterns of verse—he has remained more conservative, and his influence has been against neglect of the technical side of his art. 'Faiz has brought respectability back to grammatical writing', a friend wrote lately, and has rescued some of his juniors from a morass of incomprehensibility.[20] He himself told me some years ago that he thought the rhyme-schemes in his first volume had been too free and easy, and made young imitators careless; for this reason, and in order to give each poem a more sharply defined form, he had set himself to adhere more closely to fixed sequences. Innovation for its own sake has not attracted him; he has not translated foreign verse into Urdu, as some have done, and has shown no curiosity about possible new metres.

All this may give his mode of writing something of an old-fashioned look, by comparison with the more westernized idiom of so many writers up and down the world who have so obviously read T. S. Eliot and his successors. But such writers are apt to be intellectuals without roots in their native soil, whereas a style like that of Faiz, even though in origin feudal and aristocratic, can awaken a responsive thrill in the common man. No doubt it will be called on to make further changes, in his and other hands, as time goes on. The old symbolism may be approaching the end of its useful life, having performed a final service by helping to launch modern ideas that can now take their own poetic course. Some other time-honoured conventions have more obviously had their day. Complaints have been heard of too much antiquated phraseology, of poets shutting their eyes to the life around them, the changing seasons, the sun and wind and rain of the Panjab. Formerly the old dream-pictures of Persia and Turkestan could serve to express for Indo-Muslims their sense of being a community in, but not of, India. Now most of these Muslims have their own sub-Himalayan homeland, they may well want to hear from their poets about their own skies, flowers, lives, instead of those of the half-mythical native land of their half-mythical ancestors. To go on harping on too many old strings will be as fatal to Urdu poetry as to plunge into unintelligible modernism, and leave it to linger as a mere ghost of the past, haunting the hall of Faiz's poem where no-one will ever come any more.

Urdu and its poetry have had a strange history; what the future holds for them must be uncertain. It is not out of the question that Faiz may prove to have been the last important figure. Over the language itself a question-mark hangs, though the same is true in one sense or another of every language, including the one most used and most misused, English. Urdu began as the speech of the camp, and became that of the city, but it has still to show that it can become that of a nation, or with what functions—for Pakistan like India is and must remain a multilingual country. In the western Panjab, today its literary stronghold, there are some who are turning their minds to Panjabi as the proper medium for poetry. To hold its ground Urdu will need to show itself able to produce more, and more varied, prose, as well as poetry still able to thrill. So far, in the two decades since independence, its progress has been halting, and poetry—it seems generally agreed among those competent to judge—has not on the whole maintained the standard achieved before 1947. Some gifted writers have flagged, new talents of distinction have been few.

Of the older group, Faiz has gone on writing, and gone on developing, and now links his generation with the younger one where his most responsive hearers are to be found, captivated partly by his romantic note, partly by his idealism. Much remains for him to do; he has done enough to be looked upon as the most significant Urdu poet, in Pakistan or India, of the time since Iqbal, and he and his poems will keep their place as a strand in the history that our epoch has been weaving.

# نقشِ فریادی

# REMONSTRANCE

## *'COMPLAINING IMAGE'*

## NAQSH-E-FARYĀDĪ

# اشعار

رات یُوں دِل میں تری کھوئی ہوئی یاد آئی

جَیسے وِیرانے میں چُپکے سے بہار آجائے

جَیسے صحراؤں میں ہَولے سے چلے بادِ نسِیم

جَیسے بِیمار کو بے وجہ قرار آجائے

## 1. LAST NIGHT

Last night your faded memory filled my heart
Like spring's calm advent in the wilderness,
Like the soft desert footfalls of the breeze,
Like peace somehow coming to one in sickness.

### *VERSES*

1 *Last night your lost memory so came into the heart*
*As spring comes in the wilderness quietly,*
*As the zephyr moves slowly in deserts,*
*As rest comes without cause to a sick man.*

### ASH'ĀR

1 Rāt yūṅ dil meṅ těrī kho'ī hū'ī yād ā'ī
Jaise vīrāne meṅ chupke-se bahār ā-jā'e,
Jaise ṣaḥrāoṅ meṅ haule-se chale bād-e-nasīm,
Jaise bīmār ko be-vajh qarār ā-jā'e.

# خُدا وُہ وقت نہ لائے....

خُدا وُہ وقت نہ لائے کہ سوگ وار ہو تُو
سُکُوں کی نیند تجُھے بھی حرام ہو جائے
تِری مسرّتِ پیہم تمام ہو جائے
تِری حیات تجُھے تلخ جام ہو جائے
غموں سے آئِنۂ دِل گُداز ہو تیرا
ہُجُومِ یاس سے بے تاب ہو کے رہ جائے
وُفُورِ دردسے سِیماب ہو کے رہ جائے
تِرا شباب فقط خواب ہو کے رہ جائے
غُرُورِ حُسن سراپا نیاز ہو تیرا

## 2. GOD NEVER SEND

God never send a time when you too mourn—
When you too find life-easing sleep forsworn,
When joy has spent with you its long bright hour
And left the cup of your existence sour;

When, its bright mirror tarnished with hot tears,
Your mind is filled with swarms of anxious fears,
And thronging misery comes with gnawing tooth,
Till only an old dream is left of youth;

### *MAY GOD NOT BRING THAT TIME*

*May God not bring that time when you are sorrowful,*
*When the sleep of tranquillity becomes forbidden to you too,*
*Your uninterrupted happiness is concluded,*
*Your life becomes for you a bitter cup,*
*The mirror of your heart is melted with grief,*
*You become disquieted by a throng of despairs,*
*You become restless (like quicksilver) from a crowd of distresses,*
*Your youth becomes only a dream,*
*Your pride of beauty is altogether humbled,*

### KHUDĀ VO WAQT NA LĀ'E

Khudā vo waqt na lā'e kĕ sogwār ho tū,
Sukūṅ kī nīṅd tujhe bhī ḥarām ho-jā'e,
Tĕrī masarrat-e-paiham tamām ho-jā'e,
Tĕrī ḥayāt tujhe talkh jām ho-jā'e,
Ghamoṅ se ā'ina-e-dil gudāz ho terā,
Hujūm-e-yās se be-tāb hoke rah-jā'e,
Wufūr-e-dard se sīmāb hoke rah-jā'e,
Tĕrā shabāb faqaṭ khẉāb hoke rah-jā'e,
Ghurūr-e-ḥusn sarāpā nayāz ho terā,

طویل راتوں میں تُو بھی قرار کو ترسے
تری نگاہ کسی غمگسار کو ترسے
خزاں رسیدہ تمنّا بہار کو ترسے
کوئی جبیں نہ ترے سنگِ آستاں پہ جُھکے
کہ جنسِ عجز و عقیدت سے تجھ کو شاد کرے
فریبِ وعدۂ فردا پہ اعتماد کرے
خدا وہ وقت نہ لائے کہ تجھ کو یاد آئے
وہ دل کہ تیرے لئے بے قرار اب بھی ہے
وہ آنکھ جس کو ترا انتظار اب بھی ہے

When beauty's proud thoughts turn to abjectness,
And you too long through the long night for peace,
While parched eyes strain for comfort no-one brings
And autumn's sad desire thirsts for new springs;

When no more foreheads bowed on your doorstep find you
Have cheated with some sweet tomorrow-vow
As thanks for love's humility's display;

God never send that time that must remind you
Of the poor heart in torment for you now,
These eyes that wait and watch for you today.

*In long nights you too pant for peace,*
*Your glances pant for some comforter,*
*Autumnal longing pants for spring,*
*No forehead bends over your doorstep*
*To make you happy with its wares of submission and devotion,*
*To put faith in the deceit of a promise of tomorrow;*
*May God not bring that time when recollection comes to you*
*Of that heart which is restless for you even now,*
*That eye which is waiting for you even now.*

Ṭawīl rātoṅ meṅ tū bhī qarār ko tarse,
Tĕrī nigāh kisī g͟ham-gusār ko tarse,
Khazāṅ-rasīda tamannā bahār ko tarse,
Ko'ī jabīṅ na tĕre saṅg-e-āstāṅ pĕ jhuke
Kĕ jins-e-'ajaz-o-'aqīdat se tujh-ko shād kare,
Fareb-e-va'da-e-fardā pĕ i'timād kare;
K͟hudā vo waqt na lā'e kĕ tujh-ko yād ā'e
Vo dil kĕ tere liye be-qarār ab bhī hai,
Vo ānkh jis-ko tĕrā intiz̤ār ab bhī hai.

# سُرودِ شبانہ

نیم شب، چاند، خُود فراموشی    محفلِ ہست و بُود ویراں ہے
پیکرِ اِلتجا ہے خاموشی    بزمِ انجُم فسُردہ ساماں ہے

آبشارِ سُکوت جاری ہے
چار سُو بے خُودی سی طاری ہے

زِندگی جُزوِ خواب ہے گویا    ساری دُنیا سراب ہے گویا
سو رہی ہے گھنے درختوں پر    چاندنی کی تھکی ہُوئی آواز
کہکشاں نیم وا نگاہوں سے    کہہ رہی ہے حدیثِ شوقِ نیاز
سازِ دِل کے خموش تاروں سے    چھن رہا ہے خُمارِ کیف آگیں

آرزُو، خواب، تیرا رُوئے حسیں

## 3. NOCTURNE

Midnight, moon, oblivion—
The sum of things an emptiness,
Desire hushed into stillness,
Listless the fellowship of the stars,
A cataract of silence streaming;
Everywhere self-forgetting reigns:

## *MUSIC BY NIGHT*

*Midnight, moon, self-forgetfulness;*
*The assemblage of existence is desolate,*
*Silence is the embodiment of longing,*
*The gathering of stars is a melancholy thing,*
*The waterfall of silence is flowing,*
*On the four sides a sort of unconsciousness is prevailing.*

## SARŪD-E-SHABĀNA

Nīm-shab, chāṅd, k͟hwud-farāmoshī;
Maḥfil-e-hast-o-būd vīrāṅ hai,
Paikar-e-iltijā hai k͟hāmoshī,
Bazm-e-anjum fasurda sāmāṅ hai,
Ābshār-e-sukūt jārī hai,
Chār sū be-k͟hwudī-sī ṭārī hai.

Life, fragment of a dream—
Earth, all a shadow-play.
Slumbering in the dense woods,
Moonlight's exhausted murmur—
Eyes half-closed the Milky Way
Breathes legends of self-surrendering love;
From the heart's unplucked strings
Echoes of blissful raptures drift—
Longings, dreams, and your charmed face.

*Life is like a part of a dream,*
*All the world is like a mirage;*
*On the dense trees is sleeping*
*The tired voice of moonlight;*
*The Milky Way with half-open glances*
*Is telling stories of the passion of self-abasement* (*love*)*;*
*From the silent strings of the lyre of the heart*
*Is being diffused a blissful intoxication—*
*Longing, dream, your beautiful face.*

Zindagī juzv-e-k̲h̲ẉāb hai goyā,
Sārī dunyā sarāb hai goyā;
So-rahī hai ghane darak̲h̲toṅ par
Chāṅdnī kī thakī hū'ī āwāz;
Kahkashāṅ nīm wā nigāhoṅ se
Kah-rahī hai ḥadīṣ̤-e-shauq-e-nayāz;
Sāz-e-dil ke k̲h̲amosh tāroṅ se
Chhan-rahā hai k̲h̲umār-e-kaif-āgīṅ—
Ārzū, k̲h̲wāb, terā rū-e-ḥasīṅ.

# آج کی رات

آج کی رات سازِ دردنہ چھیڑ

دُکھ سے بھرپور دن تمام ہُوئے
اَور کل کی خبر کِسے معلُوم؟
دوش و فردا کی مِٹ چُکی ہیں حدود
ہو نہ ہو اب سحر، کِسے معلُوم؟
زِندگی ہیچ! لیکن آج کی رات
اِیزدیّت ہے مُمکِن آج کی رات
آج کی رات سازِ دردنہ چھیڑ

اب نہ دُہرا فسانہ ہائے الم
اپنی قِسمت پہ سوگوار نہ ہو
فِکرِ فردا اُتار دے دِل سے
عُمرِ رفتہ پہ اشکبار نہ ہو
عہدِ غم کی حِکایتیں مت پُوچھ
ہو چُکیں سب شِکایتیں مت پُوچھ
آج کی رات سازِ دردنہ چھیڑ

## 4. TONIGHT

Touch tonight no chord of sorrow,
Misery-laden days have ended—
Who can tell us of tomorrow?
Its and yesterday's dim frontier
Blotted out—yet who knows whether
We and dawn are close together?
Life, a nothing; but this night—
What the gods are, we can be!

## *TONIGHT*

*Tonight do not pluck the lyre of pain;*
*The grief-filled days have been accomplished,*
*And to whom is known the news of tomorrow?*
*The frontiers of last night and tomorrow have been wiped out:*
*To whom is known whether or not there will be dawn?*
*Life is nothing—but tonight!*
*Godhood is possible tonight!*

## ĀJ KĪ RĀT

Āj kī rāt sāz-e-dard na chheṛ;
Dukh se bhar-pūr din tamām hū'e,
Aur kal kī khabr kise ma'lūm?
Dosh o fardā kī miṭ-chukī haiṅ ḥudūd,
Ho na ho ab saḥar, kise ma'lūm?
Zindagī hech! lekin āj kī rāt—
Īzadīyat hai mumkin āj kī rāt.

Touch tonight no mournful strings,
Tell no tidings of affliction,
Do not pine at what fate brings:
Care of days to come all banished,
Shed no tears for seasons vanished,
Ask no tales of hours of weeping
Or of griefs in Time's safe-keeping—
Touch no mournful notes tonight!

*Tonight do not pluck the lyre of pain;*
*Do not repeat now stories of anguish—*
*Do not be mournful over your fate—*
*Lift from the heart cares of tomorrow,*
*Do not be tearful over the age gone by;*
*Do not ask for tales of the time of sorrow;*
*All lamentations are finished—ask no more;*
*Tonight do not pluck the lyre of pain!*

Āj kī rāt sāz-e-dard na chheṛ;
Ab na duhrā fasānahā-e-alam,
Apnī qismat pĕ sogwār na ho,
Fikr-e-fardā utār-de dil se,
'umr-e-rafta pĕ ashkbār na ho;
'ahd-e-gham kī ḥikāyateṅ mat pūchh;
Ho-chukíṅ sab shikāyateṅ, mat pūchh;
Āj kī rāt sāz-e-dard na chheṛ.

# ایک منظر

بام و در خامُشی کے بوجھ سے چُور    آسمانوں سے جُوئے دَرد رواں
چاند کا دُکھ بھرا فسانۂ نُور    شاہراہوں کی خاک میں غلطاں
خوابِ گاہوں میں نیم تاریکی
مُضمحل لَے ربابِ ہستی کی
ہلکے ہلکے سُروں میں نوحہ کُناں

## 5. A SCENE

On gate and roof a crushing load of silence—
From heaven a flowing tide of desolation—
The moon's pale beams, whispered regrets, lying
In pools ebbing away on dusty highroads—
In the abodes of sleep a half-formed darkness—
From Nature's harp a dying strain of music
On muted strings faintly, faintly lamenting.

### *A SCENE*

*Roof and door crushed by a weight of silence,*
*From the skies a river of pain flowing,*
*The moon's grief-filled story of light*
*Wallowing in the dust of highways;*
*In bedrooms a half-darkness,*
*Exhausted melody of the rebeck of existence*
*Sounding a lament on faint, faint notes.*

### EK MANZ̤AR

Bām-o-dar k͟hāmushī ke bojh se chūr,
Āsmānoṅ se jū-e-dard rawāṅ,
Chāṅd kā dukh-bharā fasāna-e-nūr
Shāhrāhoṅ kī k͟hāk meṅ g͟halṭāṅ,
K͟hwābgāhoṅ meṅ nīm tārīkī,
Muẓmaḥil lai rabāb-e-hastī kī
Halke halke suroṅ meṅ nauḥa-kunāṅ!

# مجھ سے پہلی سی محبّت مری محبُوب نہ مانگ

مُجھ سے پہلی سی محبت مری محبُوب نہ مانگ

مَیں نے سمجھا تھا کہ تُو ہے تو درخشاں ہے حیات
تیرا غم ہے تو غمِ دہر کا جھگڑا کیا ہے
تیری صُورت سے ہے عالم میں بہاروں کو ثبات
تیری آنکھوں کے سِوا دُنیا میں رکھّا کیا ہے

تُو جو مِل جائے تو تقدِیر نگُوں ہو جائے

یُوں نہ تھا، میں نے فقط چاہا تھا یُوں ہو جائے
اَور بھی دُکھ ہیں زمانے میں مُحبّت کے سِوا
راحتیں اَور بھی ہَیں وصل کی راحت کے سِوا
اَن گنت صدیوں کے تاریک بہیمانہ طِلسم

## 6. LOVE, DO NOT ASK

Love, do not ask me for that love again.
Once I thought life, because you lived, a prize—
The time's pain nothing, you alone were pain;
Your beauty kept earth's springtimes from decay,
My universe held only your bright eyes—
If I won you, fate would be at my feet.

It was not true, all this, but only wishing;
Our world knows other torments than of love,
And other happiness than a fond embrace.
Dark curse of countless ages, savagery

### *DO NOT ASK FROM ME, MY BELOVED, LOVE LIKE THAT FORMER ONE*

*Do not ask from me, my beloved, love like that former one.*
*I had believed that you are, therefore life is shining;*
*There is anguish over you, so what wrangle is there over the sorrow of the age?*
*From your aspect springtimes on earth have permanence;*
*What does the world hold except your eyes?*
*If you were to become mine, fate would be humbled.*
*—It was not so, I had only wished that it should be so.*
*There are other sufferings of the time (world) besides love,*
*There are other pleasures besides the pleasures of union.*
*The dark beastly spell of countless centuries,*

### MUJH-SE PAHLĪ-SĪ MAḤABBAT, MĔRĪ MAḤBŪB, NA MĀṄG

Mujh-se pahlī-sī maḥabbat, mĕrī maḥbūb, na māṅg.
Maiṅ-ne samajhā thā kĕ tū hai, to darak̲h̲shāṅ hai ḥayāt;
Terā g̲h̲am hai to g̲h̲am-e-dahr kā jhagṛā kyā hai?
Terī ṣūrat se hai 'ālam meṅ bahāroṅ ko s̤abāt,
Terī āṅkhoṅ ke siwā dunyā meṅ rakkhā kyā hai?
Tū jo mil-jā'e to taqdīr nigūṅ ho-jā'e.
Yūṅ na thā, maiṅ-ne faqat̤ chāhā thā yūṅ ho-jā'e;
Aur bhī dukh haiṅ zamāne meṅ maḥabbat ke siwā,
Rāḥateṅ aur bhī haiṅ vaṣl kī rāḥat ke siwā.
An-ginat ṣadyoṅ ke tārīk bahemāna t̤ilism

ریشم و اطلس و کمخاب میں بُنوائے ہُوئے
جا بجا بکتے ہُوئے کُوچہ و بازار میں جسم
خاک میں لتھڑے ہُوئے خُون میں نہلائے ہُوئے

جسم نکلے ہُوئے امراض کے تنّوروں سے
پیپ بہتی ہُوئی گلتے ہُوئے ناسُوروں سے
لَوٹ جاتی ہے اُدھر کو بھی نظر کیا کیجے
اب بھی دِل کش ہے ترا حُسن، مگر کیا کیجے

اَور بھی دُکھ ہیں زمانے میں محبّت کے سِوا
راحتیں اَور بھی ہیں وصل کی راحت کے سِوا
مُجھ سے پہلی سی محبّت مری محبُوب نہ مانگ

Inwoven with silk and satin and gold lace,
Men's bodies sold in street and marketplace,
Bodies that caked grime fouls and thick blood smears,
Flesh issuing from the cauldrons of disease
With festered sores dripping corruption—these
Sights haunt me too, and will not be shut out;
Not be shut out, though your looks ravish still.

This world knows other torments than of love,
And other happiness than a fond embrace;
Love, do not ask for my old love again.

*Woven into silk and satin and brocade,—*
*Bodies sold everywhere in alley and market,*
*Smeared with dust, washed in blood,*
*Bodies that have emerged from the ovens of diseases,*
*Pus flowing from rotten ulcers—*
*My glance comes back that way too: what is to be done?*
*Your beauty is still charming, but what is to be done?*
*There are other sufferings of the time (world) besides love,*
*There are other pleasures besides the pleasures of union;*
*Do not ask from me, my beloved, love like that former one.*

Resham o aṭlas o kamkhāb meṅ bunwā'e hū'e,
Jā-ba-jā bikte hū'e kūcha o bāzār meṅ jism,
Khāk meṅ lithaṛe hū'e, khūn meṅ nahlā'e hū'e,
Jism nikale hū'e amrāẓ ke tannūroṅ se,
Pīp bahtī hū'ī galte hū'e nāsūroṅ se—
Lauṭ-jātī hai udhar ko bhī naẓar, kyā kīje?
Ab bhī dilkash hai tĕrā ḥusn, magar kyā kīje?
Aur bhī dukh haiṅ zamāne meṅ maḥabbat ke siwā,
Rāḥateṅ aur bhī haiṅ vaṣl kī rāḥat ke siwā;
Mujh-se pahlī-sī maḥabbat, mĕrī maḥbūb, na māṅg.

# رقیب سے

آ کہ وابستہ ہیں اُس حُسن کی یادیں تجھ سے
جس نے اِس دِل کو پری خانہ بنا رکھا تھا
جس کی اُلفت میں بُھلا رکھی تھی دُنیا ہم نے
دہر کو دہر کا افسانہ بنا رکھا تھا

آشنا ہیں تِرے قدموں سے وہ راہیں جِن پر
اُس کی مدہوش جوانی نے عِنایت کی ہے
کارواں گُذرے ہیں جن سے اُسی رعنائی کے
جس کی اِن آنکھوں نے بے سُود عِبادت کی ہے

تجھ سے کھیلی ہیں وہ محبُوب ہوائیں جِن میں
اُس کے مَلبُوس کی افسُردہ مہک باقی ہے
تجھ پہ بھی برسا ہے اُس بام سے مہتاب کا نور

## 7. TO THE RIVAL

Round you my memories of that fair one twine
Who made my heart a fairies' nursery,
Caught in whose toils I called this busy age
An old wives' tale, and let the world go by.

Familiar with your feet too are those paths
Her youthtime deigned to tread, drunk with youth's pride,
While as her beauty's pageant passed, these eyes
Gazed on it worshipping, unsatisfied.

With you too have those darling breezes played
Where fading perfume of her dress still hangs,
On you too from her roof has rained that moonlight

### *TO THE RIVAL*

*Come, for memories are linked with you of that beauty*
*Who turned this heart into a fairy-house,*
*In attachment to whom I had forgotten the world,*
*I had turned the age into a fable of an age.*
*Familiar with your steps are those paths on which*
*Her intoxicated youth bestowed itself,*
*By which the caravans of her charms have passed*
*That these eyes profitlessly adored.*
*With you have played those beloved breezes in which*
*The faded scent of her dress remains;*
*On you too has rained from that roof the light of the moon*

### RAQĪB SE

Ā kĕ vābasta haiṅ us ḥusn kī yādeṅ tujh-se
Jis-ne is dil ko parī-k͟hāna banā-rakhā thā,
Jiskī ulfat meṅ bhulā-rakkhī thī dunyā ham-ne,
Dahr ko dahr kā afsāna banā-rakhā thā.
Āshnā haiṅ tĕre qadmoṅ se vo rāheṅ jin-par
Uskī madhosh jawānī-ne 'ināyat kī hai,
Kārawāṅ guzare haiṅ jin-se usī ra'nā'ī ke
Jiskī in āṅkhoṅ-ne be-sūd 'ibādat kī hai.
Tujh-se khelī haiṅ vo maḥbūb hawā'eṅ jin-meṅ
Uske malbūs kī afsurda mahak bāqī hai;
Tujh-pĕ bhī barsā hai us bām se mahtāb kā nūr

جس میں بیتی ہوئی راتوں کی کسک باقی ہے

تُو نے دیکھی ہے وُہ پیشانی، وُہ رُخسار، وُہ ہونٹ
زِندگی جِن کے تصوّر میں لُٹا دی ہم نے
تجھ پہ اُٹھی ہیں وُہ کھوئی ہُوئی ساحر آنکھیں
تُجھ کو معلُوم ہے کیُوں عُمر گنوا دی ہم نے

ہم پہ مُشترکہ ہیں اِحسان غمِ اُلفت کے
اِتنے اِحسان کہ گِنواؤں تو گِنوا نہ سکوں
ہم نے اِس عشق میں کیا کھویا ہے کیا سِیکھا ہے

Haunted by long-done nights and bygone pangs.

You who have known that cheek, those lips, that brow
Under whose spell I fleeted life away,
You whom the dreamy magic of those eyes
Has touched, can tell where my years ran astray.

Such gifts as love and love's keen anguish bring,
Gifts beyond counting, side by side we earned:
To whom else could I speak of what that passion
Cost me, or through that passion what I learned?

*In which the pain of bygone nights remains.*
*You have seen that forehead, that cheek, that lip,*
*In contemplation of which I squandered existence;*
*On you have been raised those lost-in-thought magical eyes;*
*To you is known why I wasted life.*
*Ours in partnership are the favours of the pain of devotion,*
*So many favours that if I were to count I would not be able to count;*
*What I lost in this love, what I learned,*

Jis-meṅ bītī hū'ī rātoṅ kī kasak bāqī hai;
Tū-ne dekhī hai vo peshānī, vo rukhsār, vo hoṅṭ
Zindagī jinke taṣawwur meṅ luṭā-dī ham-ne,
Tujh-pĕ uṭṭhī haiṅ vo khō'ī hū'ī sāḥir āṅkheṅ,
Tujhko ma'lūm hai kyūṅ 'umr gaṅwā-dī ham-ne.
Ham-pĕ mushtaraka haiṅ iḥsān gham-e-ulfat ke,
Itne iḥsān ke ginwā'ūṅ to ginwā na sakūṅ;
Ham-ne is 'ishq meṅ kyā khoyā hai, kyā sīkhā hai,

جُز ترے اور کو سمجھاؤں تو سمجھا نہ سکوں

عاجزی سیکھی، غریبوں کی حمایت سیکھی،
یاس و حرمان کے، دُکھ درد کے معنی سیکھے
زیردستوں کے مصائب کو سمجھنا سیکھا
سرد آہوں کے، رُخِ زرد کے معنی سیکھے

جب کہیں بیٹھ کے روتے ہیں وہ بے کس جن کے
اشک آنکھوں میں بلکتے ہوئے سو جاتے ہیں
ناتوانوں کے نوالوں پہ جھپٹتے ہیں عقاب
بازو تولے ہوئے منڈلاتے ہوئے آتے ہیں

I learned of misery, helplessness, despair,
I learned to be the friend of suffering creatures,
I came to know the torment of the oppressed,
The truth of sobbing breath and livid features.

Wherever now the friendless crouch and wail
Till in their eyes the trickling tears grow cold,
Or where the vulture hovering on broad pinions
Snatches the morsel from their feeble hold—

*If I were to explain to anyone except you I would not be able to explain.*
*I learned helplessness, I learned protection of the poor;*
*I learned the meaning of despair and frustration, of suffering and pain,*
*I learned to understand the afflictions of the downtrodden,*
*I learned the meaning of chill sighs, of livid faces.*
*Wherever sitting weep those helpless ones whose*
*Tears, flowing in their eyes, fall asleep—*
*Or eagles pounce on the morsels of the feeble ones,*
*As they come spreading their wings, hovering,—*

Juz tĕre aur ko samjhā'ūṅ to samjhā na sakūṅ.
ʻājizī sīkhī, g̲h̲arīboṅ kī ḥimāyat sīkhī,
Yās o ḥirmān ke, dukh dard ke maʻnī sīkhe,
Zerdastoṅ ke maṣā'ib ko samajhnā sīkhā,
Sard āhoṅ ke, ruk̲h̲-e-zard ke maʻnī sīkhe.
Jab kahīṅ baiṭhke rote haiṅ vo be-kas jinke
Ashk āṅkhoṅ meṅ bilakte hū'e so-jāte haiṅ,
Nā-tawānoṅ ke nivāloṅ pĕ jhapaṭte haiṅ ʻuqāb
Bāzū tole hū'e, manḍlāte hū'e āte haiṅ,

جب کبھی بِکتا ہے بازار میں مزدور کا گوشت
شاہراہوں پہ غریبوں کا لہو بہتا ہے
آگ سی سینے میں رہ رہ کے اُبلتی ہے نہ پوچھ
اپنے دِل پر مجھے قابو ہی نہیں رہتا ہے

When labourers' flesh is sold in chaffering streets,
Or pavements run with poor men's blood, a flame
That lurks inside me blazes up beyond
All power of quenching; do not ask its name.

*Wherever the workman's flesh is sold in the market,*
*The blood of the poor flows on the highroads,—*
*Something like a fire that is always in my breast mounts up, do not ask!*
*No control over my heart is left to me.*

Jab kabhī biktā hai bāzār meṅ mazdūr kā gosht,
Shāhrāhoṅ pĕ g͟harīboṅ kā lahū bahtā hai,
Āg-sī sīne meṅ rah-rahke ubalti hai, na pūchh!
Apne dil par mujhe qābū hī nahīṅ rahtā hai.

# تنہائی

پھر کوئی آیا دلِ زار! نہیں کوئی نہیں
راہ رَو ہو گا، کہیں اَور چلا جائے گا
ڈھل چُکی رات، بکھرنے لگا تاروں کا غبار
لڑکھڑانے لگے اَیوانوں میں خوابیدہ چراغ
سو گئی راستہ تک تک کے ہر اِک راہ گُذار
اجنبی خاک نے دُھندلا دِئیے قدموں کے سُراغ
گُل کرو شمعیں، بڑھا دو مے و مینا و ایاغ
اپنے بے خواب کواڑوں کو مُقفّل کر لو
اب یہاں کوئی نہیں، کوئی نہیں آئے گا!

## 8. SOLITUDE

Someone has come at last, sad heart!—No, no-one is there;
A traveller must be going by, bound some other way.
The starry maze is wavering, night sinks to its decline,
About the halls the nodding lamps gutter and go out;
Each highroad slumbers, tired with long listening for steps,
An alien dust has buried deep every trace of feet.
Put out those candles, take away wine and flask and cup,
Close your high doors that know no sleep, fasten bolt and bar;
No-one, no-one will come here now, no-one any more.

### *SOLITUDE*

*Again someone has come, sad heart! No, nobody;*
*It will be a traveller, he will be going somewhere else.*
*Night has declined, the cloud of stars has begun to scatter;*
*In the halls the sleepy lamps have begun to waver.*
*Every road after long expectancy has gone to sleep;*
*Alien dust has made indistinct the traces of footsteps.*
*Put out the candles, remove wine and flagon and cup,*
*Lock up your sleepless portals.*
*Now no-one, no-one will come here!*

### TANHĀ'Ī

Phir ko'ī āyā, dil-e-zār! nahīṅ, ko'ī nahīṅ;
Rāh-rau hogā, kahíṅ aur chalā-jā'egā.
Ḍhal-chukī rāt, bikharne-lagā tāroṅ kā ghubār,
Laṛkhaṛāne-lage aiwānoṅ meṅ khẉābīda charāgh,
So-ga'ī rāsta tak-takke har-ĕk rāh-guzār;
Ajnabī khāk-ne ḍhundlā-diye qadmoṅ ke surāgh.
Gul karo sham'īn, baṛhā-do mai o mīnā o ayāgh,
Apne be-khẉāb kivāroṅ ko muqaffal kar-lo;
Ab yahāṅ ko'ī nahīṅ, ko'ī nahīṅ ā'egā!

# چند روز اَور مِری جان!

چند روز اَور مِری جان! فقط چند ہی روز
ظُلم کی چھاؤں میں دم لینے پہ مجبُور ہَیں ہم
اَور کُچھ دیر سِتم سہہ لیں، تڑپ لیں، رو لیں
اپنے اجداد کی میراث ہَے معذُور ہَیں ہم
جِسم پر قید ہَے، جذبات پہ زنجیریں ہَیں
فِکر محبُوس ہَے، گُفتار پہ تعزیریں ہَیں
اپنی ہِمّت ہَے کہ ہم پھر بھی جیئے جاتے ہَیں
زِندگی کیا کِسی مُفلِس کی قبا ہَے جِس میں
ہر گھڑی درد کے پیوند لگے جاتے ہَیں
لیکِن اب ظُلم کی میعاد کے دِن تھوڑے ہَیں
اِک ذرا صبر، کہ فریاد کے دِن تھوڑے ہَیں

## 9. A FEW DAYS MORE

Only a few days, dear one, a few days more.
Here in oppression's shadows condemned to breathe,
Still for a while we must suffer, and weep, and endure
What our forefathers, not our own faults, bequeath—
Fettered limbs, our feelings held on a chain,
Minds in bondage, and words each watched and set down;
Courage still nerves us, or how should we still live on,
Now when existence is only a beggar's gown
Tattered and patched every hour with new rags of pain?

Yes, but to tyranny not many hours are left now;
Patience, few hours of complaint are left us to bear.

### *A FEW DAYS MORE, MY DEAR!*

*A few days more, my dear, only a few days.*
*We are compelled to draw breath in the shadows of tyranny;*
*For a while longer let us bear oppression, and quiver, and weep:*
*It is our ancestors' legacy, we are blameless;*
*On our body is the fetter, on our feelings are chains,*
*Our thoughts are captive, on our speech are censorings;*
*It is our courage that even then we go on living.*
*Is life some beggar's gown, on which*
*Every hour patches of pain are fixed?*
*But now the days of the span of tyranny are few;*
*Patience one moment, for the days of complaining are few.*

### CHAND ROZ AUR, MĔRĪ JĀN!

Chaṅd roz aur, mĕrī jān! faqaṭ chaṅd-hī roz.
Ẓulm kī chhā'oṅ meṅ dam łene pĕ majbūr haiṅ ham;
Aur kuchh der sitam sah-leṅ, taṛap-leṅ, ro-leṅ.
Apne ajdād kī mīrāṣ hai, ma'zūr haiṅ ham,
Jism par qaid hai, jaẕbāt pĕ zanjīreṅ haiṅ,
Fikr maḥbūs hai, guftār pĕ ta'zīreṅ haiṅ—
Apnī himmat hai kĕ ham phir bhi jiye-jāte haiṅ.
Zindagī kyā kisī muflis kī qabā hai jis-meṅ
Har ghaṛī dard ke paiwand lage-jāte haiṅ?
Lekin ab ẓulm kī mī'ād ke din thoṛe haiṅ,
Ĕk ẕarā ṣabr, kĕ faryād ke din thoṛe haiṅ.

عرصۂ دہر کی جُھلسی ہوئی ویرانی میں

ہم کو رہنا ہے پہ یوں ہی تو نہیں رہنا ہے

اجنبی ہاتھوں کا بے نام گراں بار ستم

آج سہنا ہے، ہمیشہ تو نہیں سہنا ہے

یہ ترے حُسن سے لپٹی ہوئی آلام کی گرد

اپنی دو روزہ جوانی کی شکستوں کا شُمار

چاندنی راتوں کا بے کار دہکتا ہوا درد

دِل کی بے سُود تڑپ، جسم کی مایُوس پُکار

چند روز اَور مری جان، فقط چند ہی روز

In these close bounds of an age that desert sands choke
We must stay now—not for ever and ever stay!
Under this load beyond words of a foreign yoke
We must bow down for a time—not for ever bow!
Dust of affliction that clings to your beauty today,
Crosses unnumbered that mar youth's few mornings, soon
gone,
Torment of silver nights that can find no cure,
Heartache unanswered, the body's long cry of despair—
Only a few days, dear one, a few days more.

*In the scorched desert of the space of this age*
*We must stay, but not stay like this;*
*The nameless, heavy oppression of foreign hands*
*Today must be borne, but not always borne.*
*The dust of tribulations enfolding your beauty,*
*Counting of the frustrations of our youth of two days,*
*Futile burning pain of moonlit nights,*
*The heart's profitless throbbing, the body's despairing cry—*
*A few days more, my dear, only a few days.*

'arṣa-e-dahr kī jhulsī hū'ī vīrānī meṅ
Hamko rahnā hai pĕ yūṅ-hī to nahīṅ rahnā hai;
Ajnabī hāthoṅ kā be-nām girāṅbār sitam
Āj sahnā hai, hamesha to nahīṅ sahnā hai.
Ye tĕre ḥusn se lipṭī hū'ī ālām kī gard,
Apnī do roza jawānī kī shikastoṅ kā shumār,
Chāṅdnī rātoṅ kā be-kār dahaktā hū'ā dard,
Dil kī be-sūd taṛap, jism kī māyūs pukār—
Chaṅd roz aur, mĕrī jān! faqaṯ chaṅd-hī roz.

# کُتّے

یہ گلیوں کے آوارہ بے کار کُتّے
کہ بخشا گیا جن کو ذوقِ گدائی
زمانے کی پھٹکار سرمایہ اُن کا
جہاں بھر کی دھتکار اُن کی کمائی
نہ آرام شب کو نہ راحت سویرے
غلاظت میں گھر نالیوں میں بسیرے
جو بگڑیں تو اک دُوسرے سے لڑادو
ذرا ایک روٹی کا ٹکڑا دِکھا دو
یہ ہر ایک کی ٹھوکریں کھانے والے
یہ فاقوں سے اُکتا کے مرجانے والے
یہ مظلُوم مخلُوق گر سر اُٹھائے
تو اِنسان سب سرکشی بھُول جائے
یہ چاہیں تو دُنیا کو اپنا بنالیں
یہ آقاؤں کی ہڈّیاں تک چبالیں
کوئی اِن کو اِحساسِ ذِلّت دِلا دے
کوئی اِن کی سوئی ہوئی دُم ہِلا دے

## 10. DOGS

With fiery zeal endowed—to beg,
They roam the street on idle leg,
And earn and own the general curse,
The abuse of all the universe;
At night no comfort, at dawn no banquet,
Gutter for lodging, mud for blanket.
Whenever you find them any bother,
Show them a crust—they'll fight each other,
Those curs that all and sundry kick,
Destined to die of hunger's prick.

## *DOGS*

*These wandering unemployed dogs of the streets,*
*On whom has been bestowed ardour for beggary,*
*The curses of the age their property,*
*The abuse of the whole world their earnings,—*
*Neither rest at night nor comfort in the morning,*
*Dwellings in the dirt, night-lodgings in the drains;—*
*If they rebel, make one fight another,*
*Just show them a piece of bread—*
*They who suffer the kicks of everyone,*
*Who will die worn out with starvation.*

## KUTTE

Ye galyoṅ ke āwāra be-kār kutte,
Kĕ bakhshā-gayā jinko ẓauq-e-gadā'ī,
Zamāne kī phiṭkār sarmāya unkā,
Jahāṅ bhar kī dhatkār unkī kamā'ī,
Na ārām shab ko na rāḥat sawere,
Ghilāẓat meṅ ghar, nālyoṅ meṅ basere;
Jo bigṛeṅ to ĕk dūsre se laṛā-do,
Zarā ek roṭī kā ṭukṛā dikhā-do—
Ye harek kī ṭhokareṅ khānewāle,
Ye fāqoṅ se uktāke mar-jānewāle.

—If those whipped creatures raised their heads,
Man's insolence would be pulled to shreds:
Once roused, they'ld make this earth their own,
And gnaw their betters to the bone—
If someone made their misery itch,
Just gave their sluggish tails a twitch!

*—If these oppressed creatures lifted their heads,*
*Mankind would forget all its insolence;*
*If they wished they would make the earth their own,*
*They would chew even the bones of the masters—*
*If only someone showed them consciousness of degradation,*
*If only someone shook their sleeping tails!*

Ye maz̤lūm makh̲lūq gar sar uṭhā'e,
To insān sab sarkashī bhūl-jā'e;
Ye chāheṅ to dunyā ko apnā banā-leṅ,
Ye āqā'oṅ kī haḍḍiyāṅ tak chabā-leṅ—
Ko'ī inko iḥsās-e-ẕillat dilā-de,
Ko'ī inkī so'ī hū'ī dum hilā-de.

# بول

بول، کہ لب آزاد ہیں تیرے
بول، زباں اب تک تیری ہے
تیرا سُتواں جسم ہے تیرا
بول کہ جاں اب تک تیری ہے
دیکھ کہ آہن گر کی دُکاں میں
تُند ہیں شُعلے سُرخ ہے آہن
کُھلنے لگے قُفلوں کے دہانے
پھیلا ہر اِک زنجیر کا دامن

## 11. SPEAK

Speak, for your two lips are free;
Speak, your tongue is still your own;
This straight body still is yours—
Speak, your life is still your own.

See how in the blacksmith's forge
Flames leap high and steel glows red,
Padlocks opening wide their jaws,
Every chain's embrace outspread!

### *SPEAK*

*Speak, for your lips are free;*
*Speak, your tongue is still yours,*
*Your upright body is yours—*
*Speak, your life is still yours.*
*See how in the blacksmith's shop*
*The flames are hot, the iron is red,*
*Mouths of locks have begun to open,*
*Each chain's skirt has spread wide.*

### BOL

Bol, kĕ lab āzād haiṅ tere:
Bol, zabāṅ ab tak terī hai,
Terā sutwāṅ jism hai terā—
Bol, kĕ jāṅ ab tak terī hai.
Dekh kĕ āhangar kī dukāṅ meṅ
Tuṅd haiṅ shu'le, surkh hai āhan,
Khulne-lage qufloṅ ke dahāne,
Phailā harĕk zanjīr kā dāman.

بول ، یہ تھوڑا وقت بہت ہے
جسم و زباں کی موت سے پہلے
بول، کہ سچ زندہ ہے اب تک
بول، جو کچھ کہنا ہے کہہ لے !

Time enough is this brief hour
Until body and tongue lie dead;
Speak, for truth is living yet—
Speak whatever must be said.

*Speak, this little time is plenty*
*Before the death of body and tongue:*
*Speak, for truth is still alive—*
*Speak, say whatever is to be said.*

Bol, ye thoṛā waqt bahut hai,
Jism o zabāṅ kī maut se pahle:
Bol, kĕ sach ziṅda hai ab tak—
Bol, jo kuchh kahnā hai kah-le!

# موضوعِ سُخن

گُل ہُوئی جاتی ہے افسُردہ سُلگتی ہُوئی شام
دُھل کے نِکلے گی ابھی چشمۂ مہتاب سے رات
اَور ——— مُشتاق نِگاہوں کی سُنی جائے گی
اَور —— اُن ہاتھوں سے مس ہوں گے یہ ترسے ہُوئے ہات
اُن کا آنچل ہے، کہ رُخسار، کہ پیراہن ہے
کُچھ تو ہے جِس سے ہُوئی جاتی ہے چِلمن رنگیں
جانے اُس زُلف کی مَوہُوم گھنی چھاؤں میں
ٹِمٹِماتا ہے وُہ آویزہ ابھی تک کہ نہیں
آج پھر حُسنِ دِل آرا کی وُہی دھج ہو گی
وُہی خوابیدہ سی آنکھیں وُہی کاجل کی لکیر

## 12. POETRY'S THEME

Twilight is burning out and turning chill,
Night comes fresh-bathed from where the moon's spring
flows;
And now—these eager eyes shall have their will,
These avid fingers feel the touch of those!

Is that her fringed veil, is it her face, her dress,
Behind the hanging gauze, that makes it glow—
And in the vague mist of that rippling tress
Does the bright earring twinkle still, or no?

Subtly once more her loveliness will speak,
Those pencilled lids, those languorous eyes, again;

## *POETRY'S THEME*

*Evening, numb and smouldering, is being extinguished,*
*Soon night will emerge, bathed, from the fountain of the moon,*
*And the eyes' desire will be fulfilled,*
*And these thirsting hands will touch those hands!*
*Is it the border of her veil, or cheek, or is it her mantle?*
*Something there is by which the curtain is being tinged with colour.*
*There is no knowing whether in the hazy thick shade of that tress*
*That earring is still twinkling or not.*
*Today again there will be the same style of captivating beauty,*
*Those same as-if-sleeping eyes, that line of lampblack,*

## MAUẒŪ'-E-SUKHAN

Gul hū'ī-jātī hai afsurda sulagtī hū'ī shām,
Dhulke niklegī abhī chashma-e-mahtāb se rāt,
Aur—mushtāq nigāhoṅ kī sunī-jā'egī,
Aur—un hāthoṅ se mas hoṅge ye tarse hū'e hāt!
Unkā ānchal hai, kĕ rukhsār, kĕ pairāhan hai?
Kuchh to hai jis-se hū'ī-jātī hai chilman raṅgīṅ.
Jāne us zulf kī mauhūm ghanī chhā'oṅ meṅ
Ṭimṭimātā hai vo āweza abhī tak kĕ nahīṅ.
Āj phir ḥusn-e-dilārā kī vuhī dhaj hogī,
Vuhī khẉābīda-sī āṅkheṅ, vuhī kājal kī lakīr,

رنگِ رُخسار پہ ہلکا سا وُہ غازے کا غُبار
صندلی ہاتھ پہ دُھندلی سی حنا کی تحریر
اپنے افکار کی، اشعار کی دُنیا ہے یہی
جانِ مضموں ہے یہی، شاہدِ معنیٰ ہے یہی
آج تک سُرخ وسیہ صدیوں کے سائے کے تلے
آدم و حوّا کی اولاد پہ کیا گذری ہے؟
مَوت اور زیست کی روزانہ صف آرائی میں
ہم پہ کیا گُذرے گی، اجداد پہ کیا گذری ہے؟
اِن دمکتے ہُوئے شہروں کی فراواں مخلُوق
کیُوں فقط مرنے کی حسرت میں جیا کرتی ہے؟
یہ حسیں کھیت، پھٹا پڑتا ہے جوبن جن کا
کِس لئے اُن میں فقط بھوک اُگا کرتی ہے؟

Dusted with that faint powder, her pink cheek,
On her pale hand the henna's delicate stain.
Here is the chosen world of rhyme and dream
My muse inhabits, here her darling theme!

—Under the black and blood-red murk of ages
How has it fared with Eve's sons all these years?
How shall *we* fare, where daily combat rages
Of death with life? how fared our forefathers?

Why must those gay streets' swarming progeny
So draw breath that to die is all they crave?
In those rich fields bursting with bounty, why
Must no ripe harvest except hunger wave?

*On the colour of the cheek that faint cloud of powder,*
*On the sandalwood-coloured hand the misty tracery of henna.*
*This only is the world of my thoughts, my verses,*
*This only is the soul of my meaning, this only is the darling of my intent.*

*Down to today, under the shadow of red and black centuries,*
*What has befallen the offspring of Adam and Eve?*
*In the daily battle-array of death and life,*
*What will befall us, what has befallen our ancestors?*
*The multitudinous creatures of these glittering cities,*
*Why do they keep living only in desire of death?*
*These lovely fields, whose bloom is bursting out,*
*Why does only hunger keep growing in them?*

Raṅg-e-rukhsār pĕ halkā-sā vo ghāze kā ghubār,
Ṣaṅdalī hāth pĕ dhuṅdlī-sī ḥinā kī taḥrīr.
Apne afkār kī, ash'ār kī dunyā hai yĕhī,
Jān-e-maẓmūṅ hai yĕhī, shāhid-e-ma'nā hai yĕhī.

Āj tak surkh o siya ṣadyoṅ ke sā'e ke tale,
Ādam o Ḥavvā kī aulād pĕ kyā guzrī hai?
Maut aur zīst kī rozāna ṣafārā'ī meṅ,
Ham pĕ kyā guzregī, ajdād pĕ kyā guzrī hai?
In damakte hū'e shahroṅ kī farāwāṅ makhlūq
Kyūṅ faqaṭ marne kī ḥasrat meṅ jiyā-kartī hai?
Ye ḥasīṅ khet, phaṭā-parṭā hai joban jinkā,
Kis-liye un-meṅ faqaṭ bhūk ugā-kartī hai?

یہ ہر اِک سِمت پُراسرار کڑی دِیواریں
جل بُجھے جِن میں ہزاروں کی جوانی کے چراغ
یہ ہر اِک گام پہ اُن خوابوں کی مقتل گاہیں
جِن کے پرتَو سے چَراغاں ہَیں ہزاروں کے دماغ
یہ بھی ہَیں، اَیسے کئی اَور بھی مضموں ہوں گے
لیکن اُس شوخ کے آہستہ سے کُھلتے ہُوئے ہونٹ
ہائے اُس جِسم کے کمبخت دِل آویز خطُوط
آپ ہی کہیے کہیں اَیسے بھی افسُوں ہوں گے
اپنا موضُوعِ سُخن اِن کے سِوا اَور نہیں
طبعِ شاعِر کا وطن اِن کے سِوا اَور نہیں

Walls dark with secrets frown on every side,
That countless lamps of youth have sunk behind;
Everywhere scaffolds on which dreams have died
That lit unnumbered candles in man's mind.

—These too are subjects; more there are;—but oh,
Those limbs that curve so fatally ravishingly!
Oh that sweet wretch, those lips parting so slow—
Tell me where else such witchery could be!
No other theme will ever fit my rhyme;
Nowhere but here is poetry's native clime.

*These harsh walls on every side, full of mysteries,*
*In which the lamps of the youth of thousands have burned away,*
*These execution-grounds, at every step, of those dreams*
*By whose radiance the minds of thousands are lamps:*
*These also are themes, others also like them there may be.*
*But the slowly opening lips of that saucy one!*
*Ah, the cursed alluring lines of that body!*
*You yourself say, will there be such sorceries anywhere else?*
*My theme of poetry is nothing else except these,*
*The native land of the poet's nature is nothing else except these.*

Ye harĕk simt pur-asrār kaṛī dīwāreṅ,
Jal-bujhe jin-meṅ hazāroṅ kī jawānī ke charāgh,
Ye harĕk gām pĕ un khẉāboṅ kī maqtal-gāheṅ,
Jinke partau se charāghāṅ haiṅ hazāroṅ ke dimāgh:
Ye bhī haiṅ, aise ka'ī aur bhī maẓmūṅ hoṅge;
Lekin us shokh ke āhista-se khulte-hū'e hoṅṭ,
Hā'e us jism ke kambakht dil-āwez khut̤ūt̤—
Āp-hī kahiye, kahīṅ aise bhī afsūṅ hoṅge?
Apnā mauẓū'-e-sukhan inke siwā aur nahīṅ,
T̤ab'-e-shā'ir kā wat̤an inke siwā aur nahīṅ.

# ہم لوگ

دِل کے اَیواں میں لئے گُل شُدہ شمعوں کی قطار
نُورِ خُورشید سے سہمے ہُوئے اُکتائے ہُوئے
حُسنِ محبُوب کے سیّال تصوّر کی طرح
اپنی تاریکی کو بھینچے ہُوئے، لپٹائے ہُوئے

غایتِ سُود و زِیاں، صُورتِ آغاز و مآل
وُہی بے سُود تجسّس، وُہی بے کار سوال

## 13. OUR KIND

In the mind's hall, holding each his dead lamp,
Turning with trembling nausea from the sun's light,
Huddled in our own darkness, hugging it tight
As if in an endless dream of a sweet face;
—Riddle of good and ill and beginning and end,
The old futile inquisition, profitless chase;

### *WE*

*In the hall of the heart, bearing a row of extinguished candles,*
*Timorous of the sun's light, desponding,—*
*As if it were the flowing fantasy of a beloved beauty*
*Hugging, clinging to our own darkness;*
*Purpose of profit and loss, appearance of beginning and end,*
*The same profitless enquiry, the same useless question;*

### HAM LOG

Dil ke aiwāṅ meṅ liye gul-shuda sham'oṅ kī qat̤ār,
Nūr-e-<u>kh</u>ẉurshīd se sahme hū'e, uktā'e hū'e,
Ḥusn-e-maḥbūb ke saiyāl taṣawwur kī t̤araḥ,
Apnī tārīkī ko bhīnche hū'e, lipṭā'e hū'e;
<u>Gh</u>āyat-e-sūd-o-ziyāṅ, ṣūrat-e-ā<u>gh</u>āz-o-m'āl,
Vuhī be-sūd tajassus, vuhī be-kār sawāl,

مُضمحِل ساعتِ اِمروز کی بے رنگی سے
یادِ ماضی سے غمیں، دہشتِ فردا سے نڈھال
تِشنہ افکار جو تسکِین نہیں پاتے ہیں
سوختہ اشک جو آنکھوں میں نہیں آتے ہیں
اِک کڑا درد کہ جو گیت میں ڈھلتا ہی نہیں
دِل کے تاریک شگافوں سے نکلتا ہی نہیں
اور اِک اُلجھی ہُوئی مَوہُوم سی درماں کی تلاش
دشت وُ زِنداں کی ہوس، چاکِ گریباں کی تلاش

Tedium of today's colourless minutes,
Goad of remembrance, chill of tomorrow's fears;
Starved thoughts that come to no comfort, blistering tears
That find no way to the eye, a numb misery
Not melting into any song or escaping
From the heart's shadowed crevices;—and a quest,
Visionary, bemused, for remedy;
A thirst for desert and dungeon, for the rent garment.

*Exhausted by the colourlessness of today's moment,*
*Saddened by remembrance of the past, paralysed by fear of tomorrow;*
*Thirsty thoughts that find no relief,*
*Burning tears that do not come into the eyes,*
*One hard pain that does not take the mould of song,*
*Does not issue from the dark crannies of the heart;*
*And a tangled, confused search for a remedy,*
*A longing for desert and prison, a search for the rent garment.*

Muẓmaḥil sā'at-e-imroz kī be-raṅgī se,
Yād-e-māẓī se g͟hamīṅ, dahshat-e-fardā se niḍhāl;
Tishna afkār jo taskīn nahīṅ pāte haiṅ,
Sok͟hta ashk jo āṅkhoṅ meṅ nahīṅ āte haiṅ,
Ĕk kaṛā daṛd kĕ jo gīt meṅ ḍhaltā hī nahīṅ,
Dil ke tārīk shigāfoṅ se nikaltā hī nahīṅ;
Aur ĕk uljhī hū'ī mauhūm-sī darmāṅ kī talāsh,
Dasht o zindāṅ kī havas, chāk-e-girībāṅ kī talāsh.

# سیاسی لیڈر کے نام

سالہا سال یہ بے آسرا، جکڑے ہُوئے ہات
رات کے سخت و سیہ سینے میں پیوست رہے
جس طرح تنکا سمندر سے ہو سرگرم ستیز
جس طرح تیتری کُہسار پہ یلغار کرے
اور اب رات کے سنگین و سیہ سینے میں
اِتنے گھاؤ ہیں، کہ جس سمت نظر جاتی ہے
جابجا نور نے اِک جال سا بُن رکھا ہے
دُور سے صُبح کی دھڑکن کی صدا آتی ہے

## 14. TO A POLITICAL LEADER

Long years those hands, unfriended and unfree,
Have clawed into night's dark unyielding breast
As straws might dash themselves against a sea,
Or butterflies assail a mountain-crest:

Till now that dark and flint-hard breast of night
Has felt so many gashes that all round,
Look where you will, is woven a web of light,
And from far off the morning's heartbeats sound.

### *TO A POLITICAL LEADER*

*Year by year these unprotected, bound hands*
*Have remained fixed in the hard, black bosom of night,*
*As a straw may be ardent in strife with the sea,*
*As a butterfly may make an attack on a mountain;*
*And now in the stony and black bosom of night*
*There are so many wounds, that whichever way the eye goes*
*Everywhere light has woven a sort of web,*
*From afar the sound of the throbbing of dawn comes.*

### SIYĀSĪ *LEADER* KE NĀM

Sāl-hā-sāl ye be-āsrā, jakṛe hū'e hāt
Rāt ke sakht o siya sīne meṅ paiwast rahe,
Jis ṭaraḥ tinkā samundar se ho sargarm-e-satez,
Jis ṭaraḥ tītrī kuhsār pe yalghār kare;
Aur ab rāt ke saṅgīṅ o siya sīne meṅ
Itne ghā'o haiṅ, kĕ jis simt naẓar jātī hai
Jā-ba-jā nūr-ne ĕk jāl-sā bun-rakhā hai,
Dūr se ṣubḥ kī dhaṛkan kī ṣadā ātī hai.

تیرا سرمایہ، تری آس یہی ہات تو ہیں!
اور کچھ ہے بھی ترے پاس؟ یہی ہات تو ہیں
تجھ کو منظور نہیں غلبۂ ظلمت لیکن
تجھ کو منظور ہے یہ ہاتھ قلم ہو جائیں
اور مشرق کی کمیں گہ میں دھڑکتا ہوا دن
رات کی آہنی میّت کے تلے دب جائے!

The people's hands have been your coat of mail,
Your wealth: what else has lent you strength, but they?
You do not wish this darkness to prevail,
Yet wish those hands lopped off, and the new day,

Now throbbing in its eastern ambush, doomed
Under night's iron corpse to lie entombed.

*Your wealth, your hope, are these same hands—*
*Have you anything else?—it is these same hands.*
*You do not desire the victory of darkness, but*
*You desire that these hands be cut off,*
*And that day, throbbing in the ambuscade of the east,*
*Sink under the iron corpse of night!*

Terā sarmāya, tĕrī ās yĕhī hāt to haiṅ!
Aur kuchh hai bhī tĕre pās? Yĕhī hāt to haiṅ.
Tujhko manẓūr nahīṅ g͟halba-e-ẓulmat, lekin
Tujhko manẓūr hai ye hāth qalam ho-jā'eṅ,
Aur mashriq kī kamīṅ-gah meṅ dhaṛaktā hū'ā din
Rāt kī āhanī maiyat ke tale dab-jā'e!

# اے دلِ بے تاب ٹھہر

تیرگی ہے کہ اُمنڈتی ہی چلی جاتی ہے
شب کی رگ رگ سے لہُو پھُوٹ رہا ہو جیسے
چل رہی ہے کچھ اس انداز سے نبضِ ہستی
دونوں عالم کا نشہ ٹوُٹ رہا ہو جیسے

رات کا گرم لہُو اور بھی بہ جانے دو
یہی تاریکی تو ہے غازۂ رُخسارِ سحر
صُبح ہونے ہی کو ہے اے دلِ بے تاب ٹھہر

## 15. OH RESTLESS HEART

Darkness an ever-deepening flood,
Night's blood gushing from every vein;
Creation's pulse flutters as though
An ecstasy of the two worlds were waning.

Let night's warm blood stream on: its shade
Is powder for the cheeks of dawn.
Daybreak is near; oh restless heart, be still.

### *OH RESTLESS HEART, WAIT*

*It is a darkness that goes on swelling,*
*As if blood were spouting from night's every vein;*
*The pulse of existence is going somewhat in this fashion*
*As if an intoxication of both worlds were failing.*
*Let night's warm blood go on flowing;*
*This darkness is the powder of the face of dawn:*
*It is just about to be morning—oh restless heart, wait.*

### AI DIL-E-BE-TĀB, THAHAR

Tīragī hai kĕ umanḍatī-hī chalī-jātī hai
Shab kī rag rag se lahū phūṭ-rahā ho jaise;
Chal-rahī hai kuchh is andāz se nabẓ-e-hastī
Donoṅ ʻālam kā nasha ṭūṭ-rahā ho jaise.
Rāt kā garm lahū aur bhī bah-jāne-do;
Yĕhī tārīkī to hai g͟hāza-e-ruk͟hsār-e-saḥar:
Ṣubḥ hone hī ko hai; ai dil-e-be-tāb, ṭhahar.

ابھی زنجیر چھنکتی ہے پسِ پردۂ ساز
مُطلقُ الحکم ہے شیرازۂ اسباب ابھی
ساغرِ ناب میں آنسو بھی ڈھلک جاتے ہیں
لغزشِ پا میں ہے پابندیٔ آداب ابھی
اپنے دیوانوں کو دیوانہ تو بن لینے دو
اپنے میخانوں کو میخانہ تو بن لینے دو
جلد یہ سطوتِ اسباب بھی اُٹھ جائے گی
یہ گراں باریٔ آداب بھی اُٹھ جائے گی
خواہ زنجیر چھنکتی ہی چھنکتی ہی رہے

Through music's veil the clanking chain,
Omnipotent yet fate's web close-drawn,
Tears into life's pure winecup running,
Feet drunk with ardour clogged by custom's bane.

But let true heaven-born madness fill
Our madmen, wine our wineshops—soon
Fate's empire shall be overthrown
And tyranny of custom fade,
Let the linked chain clank now, clank as it will.

*Still a chain clanks behind the curtain of music,*
*Of absolute power still is the scheme of cause-and-effect,*
*Into the unmixed goblet tears too go rolling,*
*On the unsteadiness of the foot there is still the tether of custom.*
*Let your madmen become truly mad,*
*Let your wineshops become truly wineshops,*
*Quickly this domination of things-as-they-are shall be removed,*
*This oppressiveness of custom shall be removed—*
*Though the chain go on rattling and rattling!*

Abhī zanjīr chhanaktī hai pas-e-parda-e-sāz,
Muṭlaq ul-ḥukm hai shīrāza-e-asbāb abhī,
Sāghar-e-nāb meṅ āṅsū bhī ḍhalak-jāte haiṅ,
Laghzish-e-pā meṅ hai pābandī-e-ādāb abhī.
Apne dīwānoṅ ko dīwāna to ban-lene-do,
Apne maikhānoṅ ko maikhāna to ban-lene-do,
Jald ye saṭwat-e-asbāb bhī uṭh-jā'egī,
Ye girāṅbārī-e-ādāb bhī uṭh-jā'egī,
Khwāh zanjīr chhanaktī-hī, chhanaktī-hī rahe.

# مِرے ہمدم مِرے دوست

گر مجھے اِس کا یقیں ہو، مرے ہمدم، مرے دوست
گر مجھے اِس کا یقیں ہو کہ ترے دِل کی تھکن
تیری آنکھوں کی اُداسی، ترے سینے کی جلن
میری دِل جوئی، مرے پیار سے مِٹ جائے گی
گر مرا حرفِ تسلّی وہ دوا ہو جس سے
جی اُٹھے پھر ترا اُجڑا ہُوا بے نُور دماغ
تیری پیشانی سے دُھل جائیں یہ تذلیل کے داغ

## 16. MY FELLOW-MAN, MY FRIEND

If I could know for certain, my fellow-man, my friend—
If I could know for certain that your heart-weariness,
That brooding in your eyes and those thoughts that sear you might
Be healed by any caring or comforting of mine;
Or if my words of solace were medicine that could bring
Revival to your stricken and shadow-haunted brain,
Wipe from your brow the wrinkles that shame and failure write,

### *MY FELLOW-CREATURE, MY FRIEND*

*If I were certain of this, my companion, my friend,*
*If I were certain of this, that the weariness of your heart,*
*The sadness of your eyes, the burning in your breast,*
*Would be removed by my sympathy, my affection;*
*If my words of consolation were that medicine through which*
*Your desolated, unlit brain would recover itself,*
*These stains of humiliation be removed from your forehead,*

### MĚRE HAMDAM, MĚRE DOST

Gar mujhe iskā yaqīṅ ho, mĕre hamdam, mĕre dost—
Gar mujhe iskā yaqīṅ ho kĕ tĕre dil kī thakan,
Terī āṅkhoṅ kī udāsī, tĕre sīne kī jalan,
Merī dil-jū'ī, mĕre pyār se miṭ-jā'egī;
Gar mĕrā ḥarf-e-tasallī vo dawā ho jis-se
Jī uṭhe phir tĕrā ujṛā hū'ā be-nūr dimāg͟h,
Terī peshānī se dhul-jā'eṅ ye taẕlīl ke dāg͟h,

تیری بیمار جوانی کو شفا ہو جائے

گر مجھے اِس کا یقیں ہو مرے ہمدم مرے دوست
روز و شب، شام و سحر، میں تجھے بہلاتا رہوں
مَیں تجھے گیت سُناتا رہوں ہلکے، شیریں
آبشاروں کے، بہاروں کے، چمن زاروں کے گیت
آمدِ صُبح کے، مہتاب کے، سیّاروں کے گیت
تجھ سے مَیں حُسن و محبّت کی حکایات کہوں
کیسے مغرُور حسیناؤں کے برفاب سے جسم
گرم ہاتھوں کی حرارت میں پگھل جاتے ہیں
کیسے اِک چہرے کے ٹھہرے ہوئے مانوس نقُوش
دیکھتے دیکھتے یک لخت بدل جاتے ہیں
کِس طرح عارضِ محبُوب کا شفّاف بلَور
یک بیک بادۂ احمر سے دہک جاتا ہے

And mend the pale consumption that wastes away your youth;—

If I knew this for certain, my fellow-man, my friend!
Day and night I would cheer you, morning and evening make
Songs and new songs to please you, honeyed, heart-quieting—
Songs of cascades and springtides and flowery meadowlands,
Of breaking dawns, of moonlight, or of the wandering stars;
Or tell you old romances of shining eyes and love,
Of beautiful proud women and bosoms cold as snow
Melting under the fervent touch of a lover's hands;
Tell how familiar features, long known by heart, may while
We watch them be transfigured in one short moment's space,
Or how the crystal whiteness of the beloved one's cheek
Will suddenly be kindled into wine's ruby glow,

*Your sickly youth be cured;—*
*If I were certain of this, my companion, my friend,*
*Day and night, evening and daybreak, I would keep entertaining you,*
*I would keep singing you songs, gentle and sweet,*
*Songs of waterfalls, of springtimes, of meadows,*
*Songs of the advent of dawn, of moonlight, of planets;*
*I would tell you stories of beauty and love,*
*Of how the ice-like bodies of proud beauties*
*Melt in the ardour of warm hands;*
*How the well-known, familiar features of some face*
*While we are watching all at once become changed;*
*How the transparent crystal of the beloved's cheek*
*Suddenly glows with red wine;*

Terī bīmār jawānī ko shifā ho-jā'e—
Gar mujhe iskā yaqīṅ ho, mĕre hamdam, mĕre dost,
Roz o shab, shām o saḥar, maiṅ tujhe bahlātā rahūṅ,
Maiṅ tujhe gīt sunātā rahūṅ, halke, shīrīṅ,
Ābshāroṅ ke, bahāroṅ ke, chamanzāroṅ ke gīt,
Āmad-e-ṣubḥ ke, mahtāb ke, saiyāroṅ ke gīt;
Tujh-se maiṅ ḥusn o maḥabbat kī ḥikāyāt kahūṅ,
Kaise maghrūr ḥasīnā'oṅ ke barfāb-se jism
Garm hāthoṅ kī ḥarārat meṅ pighal-jāte haiṅ;
Kaise ĕk chahre ke ṭhahre hū'e mānūs nuqūsh
Dekhte dekhte yak lakht badal-jāte haiṅ;
Kis ṭaraḥ 'āriz-e-maḥbūb kā shaffāf bilaur
Yak-ba-yak bāda-e-aḥmar se dahak-jātā hai;

کیسے گلچیں کے لئے جھکتی ہے خود شاخِ گلاب
کِس طرح رات کا اَیوان مہک جاتا ہے

یُوں ہی گاتا رہُوں، گاتا رہُوں، تیری خاطر
گیت بُنتا رہُوں، بَیٹھا رہُوں، تیری خاطِر
پر مرے گیت ترے دُکھ کا مُداوا ہی نہیں
نغمہ جرّاح نہیں، مُونِس و غم خوار سہی
گیت نِشتر تو نہیں، مرہم آزار سہی
تیرے آزار کا چارہ نہیں، نِشتر کے سوا
اَور یہ سفّاک مسیحا مرے قبضے میں نہیں
اِس جہاں کے کسی ذی رُوح کے قبضے میں نہیں
ہاں مگر تیرے سِوا، تیرے سِوا، تیرے سِوا

—How of herself the rose-spray leans to be plucked, and send
A breath of perfume stealing through the dark hall of night;

Such songs I would keep making, to sing you hour by hour,
Weaving new notes to charm you, sitting here by your side.
But for your rooted trouble what is my rhyming worth?
Verse is soft balm for sorrow, no surgeon to save life:
Music a salve for sickness, no lancet; and there is
No remedy for sickness like yours, except the knife—
The murderer, the redeemer, that is not in my power
Nor in the power of any that draw breath on this earth:
Any, excepting only—yourself, yourself, yourself!

*How the rose-spray bends of itself for the rose-plucker,*
*How the hall of night grows perfumed;*
*—So would I keep singing, keep singing, for your sake,*
*I would go on sitting and weaving songs for your sake.*
*But my songs are no remedy for your affliction,*
*Melody is no surgeon, even though consoling and sympathetic;*
*A song is no lancet, though it may be a lotion for sickness.*
*There is no cure for your sickness, except the lancet,*
*And this butcher-messiah is not in my power,*
*Is not in the power of any breathing thing in this world,*
*Except—yes! except yourself, except yourself, except yourself.*

Kaise gulchīṅ ke liye jhuktī hai khẉud shākh-e-gulāb,
Kis ṭaraḥ rāt kā aiwān mahak-jātā hai;
Yūṅ-hī gātā-rahūṅ, gātā-rahūṅ, terī khāṭir,
Gīt buntā-rahūṅ, baiṭhā-rahūṅ, terī khāṭir.
Par mĕre gīt tĕre dukh kā mudāvā hī nahīṅ,
Naghma jarrāḥ nahīṅ, mūnis o gham-khẉār sahī;
Gīt nishtar to nahīṅ, marham-e-āzār sahī.
Tere āzār kā chāra nahīṅ, nishtar ke siwā,
Aur ye saffāk masīḥā mĕre qabẓe meṅ nahīṅ,
Is jahāṅ ke kisī ẕī-rūḥ ke qabẓe meṅ nahīṅ,
Hāṅ magar tere siwā, tere siwā, tere siwā.

# دستِ صبا

# FINGERS OF THE WIND

*THE ZEPHYR'S HAND*

DAST-E-ṢABĀ

متاعِ لوح و قلم چھن گئی تو کیا غم ہے
کہ خُون دِل میں ڈبو لی ہیں اُنگلیاں مَیں نے
زبان پہ مُہر لگی ہے تو کیا، کہ رکھ دی ہے
ہر ایک حلقۂ زنجیر میں زباں مَیں نے

## 17. IF INK AND PEN

If ink and pen are snatched from me, shall I
Who have dipped my finger in my heart's blood complain—
Or if they seal my tongue, when I have made
A mouth of every round link of my chain?

### *STANZA*

1 *If my property of tablet and pen is taken away, what grief is it,*
*When I have dipped my fingers in the blood of the heart?*
*A seal has been set on my tongue: what of it, when I have put*
*A tongue into every ring of my chain?*

### QIṬA‘

1 Matā‘-e-lauḥ-o-qalam chhin-ga'ī to kyā gham hai,
Kĕ khūn-e-dil meṅ ḍabo-lī haiṅ uṅgliyāṅ maiṅ-ne.
Zabān pĕ muhr lagī hai to kyā, kĕ rakh-dī hai
Harek ḥalqa-e-zanjīr meṅ zabāṅ maiṅ-ne.

○

کبھی کبھی یاد میں اُبھرتے ہیں نقشِ ماضی مِٹے مِٹے سے
وُہ آزمائشِ دِل و نظر کی، وُہ قربتیں سی، وُہ فاصلے سے
کبھی کبھی آرزُو کے صحرا میں آکے رُکتے ہیں قافلے سے
وُہ ساری باتیں لگاؤ کی سی، وُہ سارے عُنواں وِصال کے سے
نِگاہ و دِل کو قرار کیسا، نِشاط و غم میں کمی کہاں کی

## 18. AT TIMES

At times, at times, in remembrance faintly old scenes reviving,
Things once so near and so far—heart-vision, eye-vision striving.

At times, at times, in desire's parched sands, caravans come halting,
With tokens laden to seal all bargains of lovers' driving.

For eye or heart what repose, what slaking of joy and anguish?

### *G̲H̲AZAL*

*Sometimes, sometimes, images of the past swell up again, very faintly, in memory,*
*Those contests of heart and sight, those as it were nearnesses and farnesses;*
*Sometimes, sometimes, in the wilderness of longing, things like caravans come and stop,*
*All those things as it were of affection, all those symbols as it were of union.*
*How can there be rest to eye and heart, where any lessening of joy and grief?*

### G̲H̲AZAL

Kabhī kabhī yād meṅ ubharte haiṅ naqsh-e-māẓī miṭe miṭe-se,
Vo āzmā'ish dil-o-naẓar kī, vo qurbateṅ-sī, vo fāṣile-se;
Kabhī kabhī ārzū ke ṣaḥrā meṅ āke ruḳte haiṅ qāfile-se,
Vo sārī bāteṅ lagā'o kī sī, vo sāre 'unwāṅ viṣāl ke se.
Nigāh o dil ko qarār kaisā, nishāṭ o g̲h̲am meṅ kamī kahāṅ kī?

وُہ جب مِلے ہَیں تو اُن سے ہر بار کی ہَے اُلفت نئے سِرے سے
بُہت گِراں ہَے یہ عَیشِ تنہا، کہیں سُبک تر کہیں گوارا
وُہ دردِ پنہاں کہ ساری دُنیا رفیق تھی جِس کے واسطے سے
تُمہیں کہو رِند و مُحتسِب میں ہَے آج شب کَون فرق اَیسا
یہ آکے بیٹھے ہَیں مَیکدے میں وُہ اُٹھ کے آئے ہَیں مَیکدے سے

Each time I see her love springs anew by some fresh contriving.

This lonely pleasure is hard to bear; that was kinder torment
When inward grief kept a bond of kinship with all men thriving.

Between stern censor and rake what gulf can be found this evening?
One left the tavern just now, the second is just arriving.

*When she meets one, every time love of her has a new beginning.*
*Very heavy is this solitary pleasure; much lighter, much more agreeable,*
*That hidden pain thanks to which the whole world was a comrade.*
*You yourself say, is there any so great difference this night between profligate and censor of morals?*
*This one has come and sat down in the wineshop, that one has got up and come from the wineshop.*

Vo jab mile haiṅ to un-se harbār kī hai ulfat na'e sire se.
Bahut girāṅ hai ye 'aish-e-tanhā, kahīṅ subuktar, kahīṅ gavārā
Vo dard-e-pinhāṅ kĕ sārī dunyā rafīq thī jis-ke wāsṭe se.
Tumhīṅ kaho rind o muḥtasib meṅ hai āj shab kaun farq aisā,
Ye āke baiṭhe haiṅ maikade meṅ, vo uṭhke ā'e haiṅ maikade se.

# صُبحِ آزادی

اگست ۱۹۴۷

یہ داغ داغ اُجالا، یہ شب گزیدہ سحر
وُہ اِنتظار تھا جِس کا، یہ وُہ سحر تو نہیں
یہ وُہ سحر تو نہیں جس کی آرزو لے کر
چلے تھے یار کہ مِل جائے گی کہیں نہ کہیں

## 19. FREEDOM'S DAWN (August 1947)

This leprous daybreak, dawn night's fangs have mangled—
This is not that long-looked-for break of day,
Not that clear dawn in quest of which those comrades
Set out, believing that in heaven's wide void

## *DAWN OF FREEDOM (August 1947)*

1 *This stain-covered daybreak, this night-bitten dawn,*
*This is not that dawn of which there was expectation;*
*This is not that dawn with longing for which*
*The friends set out, (convinced) that somewhere there would be met with,*

## ṢUBḤ-E-ĀZĀDĪ (*August* 1947)

1 Ye dāgh dāgh ujālā, ye shab-gazīda saḥar,
Vo intiz̤ār thā jis-kā, ye vo saḥar to nahīṅ,
Ye vo saḥar to nahīṅ jis-kī ārzū lekar
Chale the yār kĕ mil-jā'egī kahīṅ na kahīṅ

فلک کے دشت میں تاروں کی آخری منزل
کہیں تو ہوگا شبِ سُست موج کا ساحل
کہیں تو جا کے رُکے گا سفینۂ غمِ دل

جواں لہُو کی پُر اسرار شاہراہوں سے
چلے جو یار تو دامن پہ کتنے ہاتھ پڑے
دیارِ حُسن کی بے صبر خواب گاہوں سے
پُکارتی رہیں باہیں، بدن بُلاتے رہے
بہُت عزیز تھی لیکن رُخِ سحر کی لگن
بہُت قریں تھا حسینانِ نُور کا دامن
سُبک سُبک تھی تمنّا، دبی دبی تھی تھکن
سُنا ہے ہو بھی چُکا ہے فراقِ ظُلمت و نُور
سُنا ہے ہو بھی چُکا ہے وصالِ منزل و گام

Somewhere must be the stars' last halting-place,
Somewhere the verge of night's slow-washing tide,
Somewhere an anchorage for the ship of heartache.

When we set out, we friends, taking youth's secret
Pathways, how many hands plucked at our sleeves!
From beauty's dwellings and their panting casements
Soft arms invoked us, flesh cried out to us;
But dearer was the lure of dawn's bright cheek,
Closer her shimmering robe of fairy rays;
Light-winged that longing, feather-light that toil.

But now, word goes, the birth of day from darkness
Is finished, wandering feet stand at their goal;

*In the desert of the sky, the final destination of the stars,*
*Somewhere there would be the shore of the sluggish wave of night,*
*Somewhere would go and halt the boat of the grief of pain.*

*By the mysterious highroads of youthful blood*
*When (we) friends set out, how many hands were laid on our skirts;*
*From impatient sleeping-chambers of the dwellings of beauty*
*Arms kept crying out, bodies kept calling;*
*But very dear was the passion for the face of dawn,*
*Very close the robe of the sylphs of light:*
*The longing was very buoyant, the weariness was very slight.*
*—It is heard that the separation of darkness and light has been fully completed,*
*It is heard that the union of goal and step has been fully completed;*

Falak ke dasht meṅ tāroṅ kī ākhirī manzil,
Kahīṅ to hogā shab-e sust mauj kā sāḥil,
Kahīṅ to jāke rukegā safīna-e-gham-e-dil.

Jawāṅ lahū kī pur-asrār shāhrāhoṅ se
Chale jo yār to dāman pĕ kitne hāth paṛe;
Diyār-e-ḥusn kī be-ṣabr khwābgāhoṅ se
Pukārtī-rahīṅ bāheṅ, badan bulāte-rahe;
Bahut 'azīz thī lekin rukh-e-saḥar kī lagan,
Bahut qarīṅ thā ḥasīnān-e-nūr kā dāman,
Subuk subuk thī tamannā, dabī dabī thī thakan.
Sunā hai ho bhī chukā hai firāq-e-ẓulmat-o-nūr,
Sunā hai ho bhī chukā hai viṣāl-e-manzil-o-gām;

بدل چکا ہے بہت اہلِ درد کا دستور
نشاطِ وصل حلال و عذابِ ہجر حرام

جگر کی آگ نظر کی اُمنگ دِل کی جلن
کسی پہ چارۂ ہجراں کا کچھ اثر ہی نہیں
کہاں سے آئی نگارِ صبا کدھر کو گئی
ابھی چراغِ سرِ رہ کو کچھ خبر ہی نہیں
ابھی گرانیِ شب میں کمی نہیں آئی
نجاتِ دیدہ و دِل کی گھڑی نہیں آئی
چلے چلو کہ وہ منزل ابھی نہیں آئی

Our leaders' ways are altering, festive looks
Are all the fashion, discontent reproved;—
And yet this physic still on unslaked eye
Or heart fevered by severance works no cure.
Where did that fine breeze, that the wayside lamp
Has not once felt, blow from—where has it fled?
Night's heaviness is unlessened still, the hour
Of mind and spirit's ransom has not struck;
Let us go on, our goal is not reached yet.

*The manners of the people of suffering (leaders) have changed very much,*
*Joy of union is lawful, anguish for separation forbidden.*

*The fire of the liver, the tumult of the eye, burning of the heart,—*
*There is no effect on any of them of (this) cure for separation.*
*Whence came that darling of a morning breeze, whither has it gone?*
*The lamp beside the road has still no knowledge of it;*
*In the heaviness of night there has still come no lessening,*
*The hour of the deliverance of eye and heart has not arrived.*
*Come, come on, for that goal has still not arrived.*

Badal-chukā hai bahut ahl-e-dard kā dastūr,
Nishāṭ-e-vaṣl ḥalāl o 'aẓāb-e-hijr ḥarām.

Jigar kī āg, naẓar kī umaṅg, dil kī jalan,
Kisī pĕ chāra-e-hijrāṅ kā kuchh as̤ar hī nahīṅ.
Kahāṅ se ā'ī nigār-e-ṣabā, kidhar ko ga'ī?
Abhī charāgh-e-sar-e-rah ko kuchh khabar hī nahīṅ;
Abhī girānī-e-shab meṅ kamī nahīṅ ā'ī,
Najāt-e-dīda-o-dil kī gharī nahīṅ ā'ī;
Chale-chalo kĕ vo manzil abhī nahīṅ ā'ī.

# لوح و قلم

ہم پرورشِ لوح و قلم کرتے رہیں گے
جو دل پہ گزرتی ہے رقم کرتے رہیں گے
اسبابِ غمِ عشق بہم کرتے رہیں گے
ویرانیٔ دوراں پہ کرم کرتے رہیں گے
ہاں تلخیٔ ایّام ابھی اور بڑھے گی
ہاں اہلِ ستم مشقِ ستم کرتے رہیں گے

## 20. TABLET AND PEN

I shall not cease to feed this pen, but still
Keep record of what things pass through the soul,
Still gather means for love to work its will,
Keep green this age round which blank deserts roll.

Though these days' bitterness must grow sharper yet,
And tyrants not renounce their tyranny,

### *TABLET AND PEN*

*I will go on cherishing the tablet and pen,*
*I will go on writing down what passes over the heart,*
*I will go on collecting the attributes of the grief of love,*
*I will go on pouring bounty on the desolation of the age.*
*Yes, the bitterness of the times will grow still greater;*
*Yes, the tyrant people will go on practising tyranny;*

### LAUḤ-O-QALAM

Ham parwarish-e-lauḥ-o-qalam karte-raheṅge,
Jo dil pĕ guzartī hai raqam karte-raheṅge,
Asbāb-e-gham-e-'ishq baham karte-raheṅge,
Vīrānī-e-daurāṅ pĕ karam karte-raheṅge.
Hāṅ talkhī-e-aiyām abhī aur baṛhegī,
Hāṅ ahl-e-sitam mashq-e-sitam karte-raheṅge:

منظور یہ تلخی، یہ ستم ہم کو گوارا
دم ہے تو مداوائے الم کرتے رہیں گے

مے خانہ سلامت ہے تو ہم سرخیِ مے سے
تزئینِ در و بامِ حرم کرتے رہیں گے

باقی ہے لہو دل میں تو ہر اشک سے پیدا
رنگِ لب و رخسارِ صنم کرتے رہیں گے

اک طرزِ تغافل ہے سو وہ اُن کو مبارک
اک عرضِ تمنّا ہے سو ہم کرتے رہیں گے

I taste their bitter wrongs without regret,
But while breath lasts will nurse each malady—

While yet the tavern stands, with its red wine
Crimson the temple's high cold walls; and while
My heartblood feeds my tears and lets them shine,
Paint with each drop the loved one's rosy smile.

Let others live for calm indifferent peace;
I listen to earth's pangs, and will not cease.


*This bitterness is accepted, this tyranny is endurable to me,*
*While there is breath I will go on with the healing of pain.*
*While the wineshop is safe, with the red of wine*
10    *I will go on adorning the door and roof of the shrine;*
*While there is blood left in my heart, from each tear*
*I will go on creating colour for the lip and cheek of my idol.*
*There is a fashion of indifference: they are welcome to it—*
*There is an appeal of love's-demand, and this I will go on*
     *presenting.*


Manẓūr ye talkẖī, ye sitam hamko gavārā,
Dam hai to mudāvā-e-alam karte-raheṅge.
Maikẖāna salāmat hai to ham surkẖī-e-mai se
10   Taz'īn-e-dar-o-bām-e-ḥaram karte-raheṅge,
Bāqī hai lahū dil meṅ to har ashk se paidā
Raṅg-e-lab-o-rukẖsār-e-ṣanam karte-raheṅge;
Ek ṭarz-e-tagẖāful hai so vo unko mubārak,
Ek 'arẓ-e-tamannā hai so ham karte-raheṅge.

○

نہ پُوچھ جب سے تِرا اِنتظار کِتنا ہے
کہ جِن دِنوں سے مُجھے تیرا اِنتظار نہیں
تِرا ہی عکس ہے اُن اَجنبی بہاروں میں
جو تیرے لب، ترے بازُو، تِرا کِنار نہیں

## 21. DO NOT ASK

Do not ask how much I have longed for you
Since those lost days of longing expectation;
Your image fills these unfamiliar springs
That are not your embrace, your arms, your lips.

### *STANZA*

1 *Do not ask how great my waiting (longing) for you has been since*
*Those days since when there has been for me no waiting for (expectation of) you.*
*Your image alone is in those alien springs*
*That are not your lips, your arms, your embrace.*

### QIṬA'

1 Na pūchh jab se tĕrā intiẓār kitnā hai,
Kĕ jin dinoṅ se mujhe terā intiẓār nahīṅ;
Tĕrā-hī 'aks hai un ajnabī bahāroṅ meṅ
Jo tere lab, tĕre bāzū, tĕrā kinār nahīṅ.

○

صبا کے ہاتھ میں نرمی ہے اُن کے ہاتھوں کی
ٹھہر ٹھہر کے یہ ہوتا ہے آج دِل کو گُماں
وُہ ہاتھ ڈھُونڈ رہے ہَیں بِساطِ محفِل میں
کہ دِل کے داغ کہاں ہَیں نِشستِ درد کہاں

## 22. HER FINGERS

The softness of her fingers is in this dawn-wind's hand;
And as it stirs, the fancy comes today to my mind
That her soft hands are searching through the ranks of our friends,
To find what are their heartaches, to feel where are their wounds.

### *STANZA*

1 *In the hand of the morning breeze is the softness of her hands;*
*While it lingers, this idea comes to my mind today—*
*Those hands are seeking in the place of the gathering*
*For where the scars of the heart are, where the seat of pain.*

### QIṬA'

1 Ṣabā ke hāth meṅ narmī hai unke hāthoṅ kī;
Ṭhahar-ṭhaharke ye hotā hai āj dil ko gumāṅ
Vo hāth ḍhūṅḍ-rahe haiṅ bisāṭ-e-maḥfil meṅ
Kĕ dil ke dāgh kahāṅ haiṅ, nishast-e-dard kahāṅ.

# شورشِ بربط و نَے

## پہلی آواز

اب سعی کا اِمکاں اَور نہیں پرواز کا مضموں ہو بھی چُکا
تاروں پہ کمندیں پھینک چکے، مہتاب پہ شبخوں ہو بھی چُکا
اب اَور کِسی فردا کے لئے اِن آنکھوں سے کیا پیماں کیجے
کِس خوابِ کے جھُوٹے افسُوں سے تسکینِ دِلِ ناداں کیجے
شیرینیِ لب، خوشبُوئے دہن، اب شوق کا عنُواں کوئی نہیں

## 23. LYRE AND FLUTE

*First Voice*

No spur left now for endeavour; gone, ambition of soaring; we have done
With throwing a noose to catch the stars, with laying an ambush for the moon.
What new pledge now, what promise of fine tomorrows, should I hang before
These eyes, or with what cheating illusion comfort the foolish heart once more?
No sweetness of lip, no fragrant mouth, is any emblem of love today,

### *CLAMOUR OF LYRE AND FLUTE*

*First Voice*

*Now there is no more power of endeavour, the theme of soaring aloft has altogether ended,*
*We have finished throwing nooses over stars, the night-attack on the moon is finished.*
*Now what pledge of some other tomorrow should be made to those eyes?*
*With what dream's false magic should the ignorant heart be consoled?*
*Sweetness of lips, perfume of mouth, are no longer emblems of love;*

### SHORISH-E-BARBAṬ-O-NAI

*Pahlī āwāz*

Ab sa'ī kā imkāṅ aur nahīṅ, parwāz kā maẓmūṅ ho bhī chukā,
Tāroṅ pĕ kamandeṅ phaiṅk-chuke, mahtāb pĕ shabkhūṅ ho bhī chukā;
Ab aur kisī fardā ke liye in āṅkhoṅ se kyā paimāṅ kije,
Kis khwāb ke jhūṭe afsūṅ se taskīn-e-dil-e-nādāṅ kije?
Shīrīnī-e-lab, khwushbū-e-dahan, ab shauq kā 'unwāṅ ko'ī nahīṅ;

شادابیِ دِل تفریحِ نظر، اب زِیست کا درماں کوئی نہیں

جینے کے فسانے رہنے دو، اب اُن میں اُلجھ کر کیا لیں گے

اِک موت کا دھندا باقی ہے، جب چاہیں گے نپٹا لیں گے

یہ تیرا کفن، وُہ میرا کفن، یہ میری لحد، وُہ تیری ہے

## دُوسری آواز

ہستی کی متاعِ بے پایاں جاگیر تری ہے نہ میری ہے

اِس بزم میں اپنی مشعلِ دِل بسمل ہے تو کیا، رخشاں ہے تو کیا

No gladness of heart, no sparkling eye, is any balsam of life today.
Leave off those tales of a living world—what use to entangle us in their mesh?
Our only business is how to die, and that we may settle when we wish;
For here is my shroud, and there is yours, and there is your grave, and here is mine.

*Second Voice*

Existence with all its sumless wealth is no private estate of yours or mine:
What difference, in the hall of life, if one heart's taper be quenched or bright,

*Freshness of heart, delight of the eye, are no medicine for life now.*
*Leave those tales of living—entangled in them, what shall we gain now?*
*Only one business is left, that of death, and that we shall accomplish when we wish;*
*This is your shroud, that is my shroud, this is my grave, that is yours.*

*Second Voice*

*The boundless wealth of existence is neither your fief nor mine;*
*In this assembly if the torch of one's own heart is extinguished, what of it? if shining, what of it?*

Shādābī-e-dil, tafrīḥ-e-naẓar, ab zīst kā darmāṅ ko'ī nahīṅ.
Jīne ke fasāne rahne-do, ab un-meṅ ulajhkar kyā leṅge?
Ěk, maut kā dhandā bāqī hai, jab chāheṅge niptā-leṅge;
Ye terā kafan, vo merā kafan, ye merī laḥad, vo terī hai.

*Dūsrī āwāz*

Hastī kī matā'-e-be-pāyāṅ jāgīr těrī hai na merī hai,
Is bazm meṅ apnī mash'al-e-dil bismil hai to kyā, rakhshāṅ hai to kyā?

یہ بزمِ چراغاں رہتی ہے، اِک طاق اگر ویراں ہے تو کیا
افسردہ ہیں گر ایّام ترے، بدلا نہیں مسلکِ شام و سحر
ٹھہرے نہیں موسمِ گُل کے قدم، قائم ہے جمالِ شمس و قمر
آباد ہے وادیٔ کاکل و لب، شاداب و حسیں گلگشتِ نظر
مقسوم ہے لذّتِ دردِ جگر، موجود ہے نعمتِ دیدۂ تر
اس دیدۂ تر کا شکر کرو، اِس ذوقِ نظر کا شکر کرو
اِس شام و سحر کا شکر کرو، اِن شمس و قمر کا شکر کرو

Or one niche lack its candle, when all the place besides is ablaze with light?
Though your hours languish, they shall not see the statute of night and day repealed,
The season of roses slacken its step, the glory of moon or sun concealed.
The dell of ringlet and lip still blooms, the charmed eye wanders among fresh flowers,
Fate grants us the cherished pain of love that blesses us with its tears' hot showers:
Be thankful for all those joys of sense, be thankful for all the tears that run,
Give thanks for the break of day and evening, thanks for the rays of moon and sun.

*This assembly remains illuminated: if one niche is desolate, what of it?*
*If your days are spiritless, unchanged the law of evening and morning,*
*Unhalted the steps of the season of roses, firm the beauty of sun and moon,*
*Populous the valley of ringlet and lip, fresh and lovely the eye's garden-wandering;*
*Destined is the pleasure of the pain of the liver, present is the blessing of the wet eye:*
*Give thanks for this wet eye, give thanks for this delight of sight,*
*Give thanks for this evening and morning, give thanks for this sun and moon.*

Ye bazm charāg͟hāṅ rahtī hai, ĕk ṭāq agar vīrāṅ hai to kyā?
Afsurda haiṅ gar aiyām tĕre, badlā nahīṅ maslak-e-shām-o-saḥar,
Ṭhahre nahīṅ mausim-e-gul ke qadam, qā'im hai jamāl-e-shams-o-qamar,
Ābād hai wādī-e-kākul-o-lab, shādāb o ḥasīṅ gulgasht-e-naz̤ar,
Maqsūm hai laz̲z̲at-e-dard-e-jigar, maujūd hai ni'mat-e-dīda-e-tar:
Is dīda-e-tar kā shukr karo, is z̲auq-e-naz̤ar kā shukr karo,
Is shām-o-saḥar kā shukr karo, in shams-o-qamar kā shukr karo.

## پہلی آواز

گر ہے یہی مسلکِ شمس و قمر ، اِن شمس و قمر کا کیا ہوگا
رعنائی شب کا کیا ہوگا ، اندازِ سحر کا کیا ہوگا
جب خونِ جگر برفاب بنا ، جب آنکھیں آہن پوش ہوئیں
اِس دیدۂ تر کا کیا ہوگا ، اِس ذوقِ نظر کا کیا ہوگا
جب شعر کے خیمے راکھ ہوئے ، نغموں کی طنابیں ٹوٹ گئیں

*First Voice*

Whatever statute may govern them, what profit are sun and moon to us?
What is it to us if night is lovely or day's first coming luminous?
When all our lifeblood has turned to ice, when eyes are shuttered up with steel,
What meaning have any tears, what meaning have any joys that sense can feel?
Once poetry's high pavilion burned, its tent-rope strands of music snapped,

*First Voice*

*If there is this law of sun and moon, what (good) can come of this sun and moon?*
*What can come of the charm of night, what can come of the grace of morning?*
*When the blood of the liver has turned to ice, when the eyes have been coated with iron,*
*What can come of this wet eye, what can come of this delight of sight?*
*When the tents of poetry have become ashes, when the tent-ropes of melodies have broken,*

*Pahlī āwāz*

Gar hai yĕhī maslak-e-shams-o-qamar, in shams-o-qamar kā kyā hogā?
Ra'nā'ī-e-shab kā kyā hogā, andāz-e-saḥar kā kyā hogā?
Jab k̲h̲ūn-e-jigar barfāb banā, jab āṅkheṅ āhan-posh hū'īṅ,
Is dīda-e-tar kā kyā hogā, is ẕauq-e-naz̤ar kā kyā hogā?
Jab shĕ'r ke k̲h̲aime rākh hū'e, nag̲h̲moṅ kī ṭanābeṅ ṭūṭ-ga'īṅ,

یہ ساز کہاں سر پھوڑیں گے، اِس کِلکِ گُہر کا کیا ہوگا
جب کُنجِ قفس مسکن ٹھہرا، اور جَیب و گریباں طوق و رسن
آئے کہ نہ آئے موسمِ گُل، اِس دردِ جگر کا کیا ہو گا

## دُوسری آواز

یہ ہاتھ سلامت ہیں جب تک، اِس خُوں میں حرارت ہے جب تک
اِس دِل میں صداقت ہے جب تک، اِس نُطق میں طاقت ہے جب تک

What good is the pen that scatters pearls, or where shall the sounding harp grow rapt?
If a cage's corner must be our home, iron collar and rope our scarf and sleeve—
Whether rose-harvest comes or no, what use for a lover's heart to grieve?

*Second Voice*

While these hands keep their virtue, and while warm blood is still pulsing through these veins,
While honour holds her place in our souls and reason is sovereign in our brains,

*Where shall these lyres rhapsodize, what can come of this pen of pearls?*
*When a corner of a cage has been left as dwelling, and coat-collar and robe are iron collar and rope,*
*Whether the season of roses come or not, what can come of this pain of the liver?*

*Second Voice*

*So long as these hands are alive, so long as there is warmth in this blood,*
*So long as there is sincerity in this heart, so long as there is strength in this mind,*

Ye sāz kahāṅ sar phoṛeṅge, is kilk-e-guhar kā kyā hogā?
Jab kunj-e-qafas maskan ṭhahrā, aur jaib-o-garībāṅ t̤auq-o-rasan,
Ā'e kĕ na ā'e mausim-e-gul, is dard-e-jigar kā kyā hogā?

*Dūsrī āwāz*

Ye hāth salāmat haiṅ jab tak, is k͟hūṅ meṅ ḥarārat hai jab tak,
Is dil meṅ ṣadāqat hai jab tak, is nut̤q meṅ t̤āqat hai jab tak,

اِن طوق و سلاسِل کو ہم تُم سِکھلائیں گے شورِشِ بربط و نے
وُہ شورِش جس کے آگے زبُوں ہنگامۂ طبلِ قیصر و کَے

آزاد ہیں اپنے فِکر و عمل، بھرپُور خزِینہ ہِمّت کا
اِک عُمر ہے اپنی ہر ساعت ، اِمرُوز ہے اپنا ہر فردا
یہ شام و سحر، یہ شمس و قمر، یہ اختر و کوکب اپنے ہیں
یہ لوح و قلم، یہ طبل و علم، یہ مال و حشم، سب اپنے ہیں

Let us two teach all locks and fetters the swelling music of lyre and flute,
Music to strike the imperial drum of Caesar or Kai-khosru mute!
Our treasure-house of courage is full, in thought and action both we are free,
All our tomorrows with us today, each moment of ours a century—
That dawn, that twilight belong to us, that planet and star, that sun and moon,
That tablet and pen and banner and drum and state and glory are all are own.

*I and you will teach to these iron collars and chains the clamour of lyre and flute,*
*That clamour before which the tumult of the drum of Caesar and Kai is feeble.*
*Free are our thought and deed, full our treasury of courage,*
*Each minute of ours is a lifetime, each tomorrow of ours is today;*
*This evening and morning, this sun and moon, this star and constellation are our own,*
*This tablet and pen, this drum and standard, this wealth and pomp, are all our own.*

In ṭauq-o-salāsil ko ham tum sikhlā'eṅge shorish-e-barbaṭ-o-nai,
Vo shorish jis-ke āge zabūṅ haṅgāma-e-ṭabl-e-Qaiṣar-o-Kai.
Āzād haiṅ apne fikr-o-'amal, bharpūr k͟hazīna himmat kā,
Ěk 'umr hai apnī har sā'at, imrūz hai apnā har fardā;
Ye shām-o-saḥar, ye shams-o-qamar, ye ak͟htar o kaukab apne haiṅ,
Ye lauḥ-o-qalam, ye ṭabl o 'alam, ye māl o ḥasham, sab apne haiṅ.

○

پھر حشر کے ساماں ہُوئے ایوانِ ہوس میں
بیٹھے ہیں ذوِی العدل، گُنہ گار کھڑے ہیں
ہاں جُرمِ وفا دیکھیے کِس کِس پہ ہے ثابِت
وُہ سارے خطاکار سرِ دار کھڑے ہیں

## 24. ONCE MORE

Once more a Day of Wrath's loud din
Fills old Ambition's hall:
The doomsmen seated on this hand,
The accused there in the dock.

Now see on whose heads the heinous sin
Of honesty must fall!
There its vile perpetrators stand,
And near them stands the block.

### *STANZA*

1 *Again there have been preparations of a doomsday in the hall of ambition;*
*The justiciars are seated, the sinners are standing.*
*Yes, see against whom the crime of loyalty is proved:*
*All those miscreants are standing beside the gibbet.*

### QIṬA'

1 Phir ḥashr ke sāmāṅ hu'e aiwān-e-havas meṅ;
Baiṭhe haiṅ zavī-al-'adl, gunagār khaṛe haiṅ.
Hāṅ, jurm-e-wafā dekhiye kis kis-pĕ hai ṣ̤ābit:
Vo sāre khaṭ̤ākār sar-e-dār khaṛe haiṅ.

# طوق و دار کا موسم

روِش روِش ہے وہی اِنتظار کا موسم
نہیں ہے کوئی بھی موسم بہار کا موسم
گِراں ہے دِل پہ غمِ روزگار کا موسم
ہے آزمائشِ حُسنِ نِگار کا موسم
خوُشا نظارۂ رُخسارِ یار کی ساعت
خوُشا قرارِ دِلِ بے قرار کا موسم
حدیثِ بادہ و ساقی نہیں تو کِس مصرف
خِرامِ ابرِ سرِ کوہسار کا موسم
نصیبِ صُحبتِ یاراں نہیں تو کیا کیجیے
یہ رقصِ سایۂ سرو و چنار کا موسم

## 25. THIS HOUR OF CHAIN AND GIBBET

On every pathway broods this hour of waiting,
No hour that strikes is the longed hour of spring;
And daily cares lie heavy on our souls—
This is the touchstone hour to try love's spells.

Blest minute that brings a dear face back to sight,
Blest hour that brings rest to a restless heart!
Wine-cup and cup-filler denied, in vain
That hour when cool clouds walk across the mountain,
Or cypress or chenar leaf, when no comrades
Share with us its green hour of dancing shades.

### *THE SEASON OF MANACLE AND STAKE*

*Pathway by pathway there is that same season of waiting,*
*No season at all is the season of spring.*
*Heavy on the heart is the season of distress for daily bread,*
*It is the season of the testing of the beauty of the beloved.*
*Happy the moment of the sight of the face of a dear friend,*
*Happy the season of tranquillity in the intranquil heart!*
*When there is no question of wine and cup-bearer, of what use*
*The season of the movement of the cloud over the mountain?*
*If the company of friends is not our lot, what good*
*This season of the dance of the shadow of cypress and chenar-tree?*

### ṬAUQ-O-DĀR KĀ MAUSIM

Ravish-ravish hai vuhī intiẓār kā mausim,
Nahīṅ hai ko'ī bhī mausim bahār kā mausim.
Girāṅ hai dil pĕ gham-e-rozgār kā mausim,
Hai āzmā'ish-e-ḥusn-e-nigār kā mausim.
Khẉushā naẓāra-e-rukhsār-e-yār kī sā'at,
Khẉushā qarār-e-dil-e-be-qarār kā mausim.
Ḥadīṡ-e-bāda-o-sāqī nahīṅ, to kis maṣraf
Khirām-e-abr-e-sar-e-kohsār kā mausim?
Naṣīb ṣuḥbat-e-yārāṅ nahīṅ, to kyā kīje
Ye raqṣ-e-sāya-e-sarv-o-chanār kā mausim?

یہ دل کے داغ تو دُکھتے تھے یُوں بھی پر کم کم

کُچھ اب کے اور ہے ہِجرانِ یار کا مَوسم

یہی جُنُوں کا ، یہی طَوق و دار کا مَوسم

یہی ہے جبر، یہی اِختیار کا مَوسم

قفس سے بس میں تمُھارے تمُھارے بس میں نہیں

چمن میں آتِشِ گُل کے نِکھار کا مَوسم

صبا کی مُشتِ خُرامی تہِ کمنّد نہیں

اسیرِ دام نہیں ہے بہار کا مَوسم

بلا سے ہم نے نہ دیکھا تو اور دیکھیں گے

فرُوغِ گُلشن و صَوتِ ہزار کا مَوسم

These scars ached long ago, a little—not
As this hour does that keeps all friends apart,
This hour of chain and gibbet and rejoicing,
Hour of necessity and hour of choice.

At your command the cage, but not the garden's
Red rose-fire, when its radiant hour begins;
No noose can catch the dawn-wind's whirling feet,
The spring's bright hour falls prisoner to no net.

Others will see, if I do not, that hour
Of singing nightingale and splendid flower.


*These scars of the heart ached indeed just like this, but only a little;*
*Something different now is the season of the separation from the*
*friend.*
*This is the season of ecstasy, of manacle and stake,*
*This is the season of coercion and of choice.*
15   *The cage is in your power, but not in your power is*
*The season in the garden of the brightening of the fire of the rose.*
*The wild motion of the morning-breeze is not under a noose,*
*The season of spring is not prisoner of a snare.*
*No matter; if I have not seen, others will see*
20   *The season of the brightness of the rose-garden and of the sound*
*of the nightingale.*


Ye dil ke dāg̱ẖ to dukhte the yūṅ bhī, par kam kam,
Kuchh abke aur hai hijrān-e-yār kā mausim.
Yĕhī junūṅ kā, yĕhī ṭauq-o-dār kā mausim,
Yĕhī hai jabr, yĕhī ik̲ẖtiyār kā mausim.
15   Qafas hai bas meṅ tumhāre, tumhāre bas meṅ nahīṅ
Chaman meṅ ātash-e-gul ke nikhār kā mausim.
Ṣabā kī mast k̲ẖirāmī tah-e-kamaṅd nahīṅ,
Asīr-e-dām nahīṅ hai bahār kā mausim.
Balā se, ham-ne na dekhā to aur dekheṅge
20   Furog̱ẖ-e-gulshan o ṣaut-e-hazār kā mausim.

# سرِ مقتل

(قوّالی)

کہاں ہے منزلِ راہِ تمنّا ہم بھی دیکھیں گے
یہ شب ہم پر بھی گذرے گی، یہ فردا ہم بھی دیکھیں گے
ٹھہر اے دِل، جمالِ رُوئے زیبا ہم بھی دیکھیں گے

ذرا صیقل تو ہو لے تشنگی بادہ گُساروں کی
دبا رکھیں گے کب تک جوشِ صہبا ہم بھی دیکھیں گے
اُٹھا رکھیں گے کب تک جام و مینا ہم بھی دیکھیں گے

## 26. AT THE PLACE OF EXECUTION

We too shall see the goal of hope's long race;
Patience, my heart: night's length will pass, and we
Shall see tomorrow rise with shining face.

The drinkers' thirst once sharpened, we shall see
How long the fiery grape can be denied,
Or flask and cup kept under lock and key.

### *AT THE EXECUTION-GROUND* (*Song*)

*We too shall see where is the destination of the road of longing,*
*This night will pass over us too, we too shall see this tomorrow:*
*Be still, oh heart, we too shall see the beauty of its charming face.*
*Just let the thirst of the wine-drinkers become really sharp,*
*We too shall see how long they will suppress the fervour of the grape-wine,*
*We too shall see how long they will keep away cup and flagon.*

### SAR-E-MAQTAL (Qawwālī)

Kahāṅ hai manzil-e-rāh-e-tamannā ham bhī dekheṅge,
Ye shab ham-par bhī guzregī, ye fardā ham bhī dekheṅge:
Ṭhahr, ai dil, jamāl-e-rū-e-zebā ham bhī dekheṅge.
Ẓarā ṣaiqal to ho-le tishnagī bāda-gusāroṅ kī,
Dabā rakkheṅge kab tak josh-e-ṣahbā ham bhī dekheṅge,
Uṭhā-rakkheṅge kab tak jām-o-mīnā ham bhī dekheṅge.

صلا آتو چکے محفل میں اُس کوئے ملامت سے

کسے روکے گا شورِ پندِ بے جا ہم بھی دیکھیں گے

کسے ہے جا کے لَوٹ آنے کا یارا ہم بھی دیکھیں گے

چلے ہیں جان و ایماں آزمانے آج دِل والے

وُہ لائیں لشکرِ اغیار و اعدا ہم بھی دیکھیں گے

وُہ آئیں تو سرِ مقتل، تماشا ہم بھی دیکھیں گے

یہ شب کی آخری ساعت گراں کیسی بھی ہو ہمدم

جو اِس ساعت میں پنہاں ہے اُجالا ہم بھی دیکھیں گے

جو فرقِ صُبح پر چمکے گا تارا، ہم بھی دیکھیں گے

One challenge from that street where love must hide—
And we shall see who stops for idle saws,
Or ventured once can bear to turn aside!

Today true men go out to try their cause;
Let the adversary come with legions, meet us
At the place of death—we shall see then whose the applause.

Companion, night's last hour cannot defeat us;
We shall see yet the flame it has choked down,
The star that is to flash from morning's crown.

*Let a summons have come into the assembly from that Street of Reproach,*
*We too shall see whom the babble of futile counsel will halt,*
*We too shall see who will have strength, having gone, to return.*
*Today men of heart go to test their spirit and faith;*
*Let them bring an army of rivals and enemies, we too shall see them—*
*Let them come then to the execution-ground, we too shall see the spectacle.*
*However heavy be this last hour of night, companion,*
*We too shall see the light that is hidden in this hour,*
*We too shall see the star that will shine on the summit of morning.*

Ṣalā ā to chuke maḥfil meṅ us kū-e-malāmat se,
Kise rokegā shor-e-paṅd-e-be-jā ham bhī dekheṅge,
Kise hai jāke lauṭ-āne kā yārā ham bhī dekheṅge.
Chale haiṅ jān-o-īmāṅ āzmāne āj dil-wāle;
Vo lā'eṅ lashkar-e-aghyār-o-a'dā ham bhī dekheṅge,
Vo ā'eṅ to sar-e-maqtal, tamāsha ham bhī dekheṅge.
Ye shab kī ākhirī sā'at girāṅ kaisī bhī ho, hamdam,
Jo is sā'at meṅ pinhāṅ hai ujālā ham bhī dekheṅge,
Jo farq-e-ṣubḥ par chamkegā tārā, ham bhī dekheṅge.

ہمارے دم سے ہے کُوئے جُنُوں میں اب بھی خجِل
عبائے شَیخ و قبائے امیر و تاجِ شہی
ہمیں سے سُنّتِ منصُور و قیس زِندہ ہے
ہمیں سے باقی ہے گُل دامنی و کج کُلَہی

## 27. WHILST WE BREATHE

Whilst we breathe, still in the Street of Rapture robed
Grandee, gowned preacher, crowned king, stand abashed;
Through us God-crazed Mansur, love-crazed Majnun,
And tilted cap and gay flowered coat, live on.

### *STANZA*

1 *Through our living, in the street of ecstasy are still abashed*
*The holy man's cloak and the nobleman's robe and the royal crown;*
*Through us the tradition of Mansur and Qais is still alive,*
*Through us survive flowered-dress-wearing and cap-tilting.*

### QIṬA'

1 Hamāre dam se hai kū-e-junūṅ meṅ ab bhī khajil
'abā-e-shaikh o qabā-e-amīr o tāj-e-shahī;
Hamīṅ-se sunnat-e-Manṣūr-o-Qais zinda hai,
Hamīṅ-se bāqī hai gul-dāmanī o kaj-kulahī.

○

شفق کی راکھ میں جل بجھ گیا سِتارۂ شام
شبِ فراق کے گیسو فضا میں لہرائے

کوئی پُکارو کہ اِک عُمر ہونے آئی ہے
فلک کو قافلۂ روز و شام ٹھہرائے

یہ ضِد ہے یادِ حریفانِ بادہ پیما کی
کہ شب کو چاند نہ نکلے، نہ دِن کو ابر آئے

صبا نے پھر درِ زِنداں پہ آکے دی دستک
سحر قریب ہے، دِل سے کہو نہ گھبرائے

## 28. AMONG TWILIGHT EMBERS

In the sky, while evening's star burns out among twilight embers,
Long tresses float of the night of lovers kept apart.

Will no-one sound the march!—an age almost has passed
Since heaven allowed the caravan of day-and-night to start.

No moon come now by night, cool cloud by day, to make
Old memories of friends and boon-companions smart!

Once more the breeze comes tapping at my prison door,
Whispering—Dawn is near; teach patience to your heart.

### GHAZAL

*In the ashes of twilight the star of evening has burned away,*
*The tresses of the night of separation have waved in the sky.*
*Cry out, someone, for a lifetime has nearly passed*
*That heaven has kept the caravan of day and night standing still.*
*This is the preventative of memories of wine-measuring intimates,*
*That the moon should not come out at night nor the cloud by day.*
*The morning-breeze has come again and knocked on the prison door:*
*'Daybreak is near, tell your heart not to be agitated.'*

### GHAZAL

Shafaq kī rākh meṅ jal-bujh-gayā sitāra-e-shām,
Shab-e-firāq ke gesū fazā meṅ lahrā'e.
Ko'ī pukāro kĕ ĕk 'umr hone ā'ī hai
Falak ko qāfila-e-roz-o-shām ṭhahrā'e.
Ye ẓid hai yād-e-ḥarīfān-e-bāda-paimā kī
Kĕ shab ko chāṅd na nikale, na din ko abr ā'e.
Ṣabā-ne phir dar-e-ziṅdāṅ pĕ āke dī dastak:
Saḥar qarīb hai, dil se kaho na ghabrā'e.

# دو عشق

## (۱)

تازہ ہیں ابھی یاد میں اَے ساقیِ گُل فام
وُہ عکسِ رُخِ یار سے لہکے ہُوئے ایّام
وُہ پھُول سی کِھلتی ہوئی دِیدار کی ساعت
وُہ دِل سا دھڑکتا ہُوا اُمّید کا ہنگام

اُمّید کہ لو جاگا غمِ دِل کا نصِیبہ
لو شَوق کی ترسی ہُوئی شب ہوگئی آخر
لو ڈُوب گئے دَرد کے بے خوابِ سِتارے
اب چمکے گا بے صبر نِگاہوں کا مُقدّر

## 29. TWO LOVES

Fresh yet in memory,
Saqi, rose-sister,
Those days whose bright mirror
Reflects her face still;
Those moments like opening
Blossoms, of sight of her,
Moments like fluttering
Heartbeats, of hope for her—

Hope of fulfilment
Come to end heartache,
Hope of love's night of thirst
Ending at last:
Sinking, those sleepless
Stars that rained sorrow,
Dawning, that destined
Joy so long waited—

### *TWO LOVES*

*Fresh are still in memory, oh rose-like Saqi,*
*Those days shining by the reflection of the face of the beloved,*
*That moment of meeting, like a flower opening,*
*That time of hope, like a heart palpitating—*
*Hope that, lo! the good-fortune of the sad heart has awakened,*
*Lo, love's night of longing is over at last,*
*Lo, the sleepless stars of pain have sunk,*
*Now the destined-prize of impatient looks will shine:*

### DO 'ISHQ

Tāza haiṅ abhī yād meṅ, ai sāqī-e-gul-fām,
Vo 'aks-e-rukh-e-yār se lahke hū'e aiyām,
Vọ phūl-sī khiltī hū'ī dīdār kī sā'at,
Vo dil-sā dhaṛaktā hū'ā ummed kā haṅgām—
Ummed kĕ lo jāgā gham-e-dil kā naṣība,
Lo shauq kī tarsī hū'ī shab ho-ga'ī ākhir,
Lo ḍūb-ga'e dard ke be-khẉāb sitāre,
Ab chamkegā be-ṣabr nigāhoṅ kā muqaddar:

اِس بام سے نِکلے گا ترے حُسن کا خورشید
اُس کُنج سے پھُوٹے گی کرن رنگِ حنا کی
اِس در سے بہے گا تری رفتار کا سیماب
اُس راہ پہ پھُولے گی شفق تیری قبا کی

پھر دیکھے ہیں وُہ ہجر کے تپتے ہُوئے دِن بھی
جب فکرِ دِل وجاں میں فُغاں بھُول گئی ہے
ہر شب وُہ سیَہ بوجھ کہ دِل بیٹھ گیا ہے
ہر صُبح کی لَو تیر سی سینے میں لگی ہے

Oh, this rooftop the sun
Of your beauty will gild,
From that corner its rays
Red as henna will break,
From this doorway your steps
Like quicksilver gliding,
By that pathway your skirt,
A twilit sky, flowing!

Fevered days too
I have known, separation's
Pangs, when lament was
Smothered in anguish,
Each night's dark burden
Crushing the breast,
Each daybreak's arrow
Piercing the soul.

*From this roof the sun of your beauty will emerge,*
*From that corner will break the henna-coloured ray,*
*From this door will flow the quicksilver of your walk,*
*On that path will flower the twilight of your dress.*

*Again, I have seen also those feverish days of separation*
*When lament was forgotten in anxiety of heart and soul,*
*Every night such a black load that the heart sank,*
*Every morning's flame entered my breast like an arrow.*

Is bām se niklegā tĕre ḥusn kā khwurshīd,
Us kunj se phūṭegī kirn raṅg-e-ḥinā kī,
Is dar se bahegā tĕrī raftār kā sīmāb,
Us rāh pĕ phūlegī shafaq terī qabā kī.

Phir dekhe haiṅ vo hijr ke tapte hū'e din bhī
Jab fikr-e-dil-o-jāṅ meṅ fughāṅ bhūl-ga'ī hai,
Har shab vo siya bojh ke dil baiṭh-gayā hai,
Har ṣubḥ kī lau tīr-sī sīne meṅ lagī hai.

تنہائی میں کیا کیا نہ تجھے یاد کیا ہے
کیا کیا نہ دِلِ زار نے ڈھونڈی ہیں پناہیں
آنکھوں سے لگایا ہے کبھی دستِ صبا کو
ڈالی ہیں کبھی گردنِ مہتاب میں باہیں

(۲)

چاہا ہے اِسی رنگ میں لیلائے وطن کو
تڑپا ہے اِسی طور سے دِل اُس کی لگن میں
ڈھونڈی ہے یُونہی شوق نے آسائشِ منزل
رُخسار کے خم میں، کبھی کاکُل کی شِکن میں

Lonely, how many
Ways I remembered you—
Wretched, how many
Refuges caught at,
Pressing the wind's cool
Hand on hot eyelids,
Round the moon's cold neck
Throwing these arms!

---

So I have loved that
Mistress, my country,
Heart no less ardent
Beating for her:
This love too a pilgrim,
Seeking its haven
Now in a curving cheek,
Now a curled lock.

*In solitude what remembrances of you did I not have,*
*What refuges did the sad heart not search for;*
*Sometimes I laid on my eyes the hand of the morning-breeze,*
*Sometimes I put my arms round the neck of the moon.*

---

*In the same fashion I have loved my darling country,*
*In the same manner my heart has throbbed with devotion to her,*
*In the same way my passion has sought for the easement of a resting-place*
*In the curve of her cheek, sometimes in the curl of her ringlet;*

Tanhā'ī meṅ kyā kyā na tujhe yād kiyā hai,
Kyā kyā na dil-e-zār-ne ḍhūṅḍī haiṅ panâheṅ;
Āṅkhoṅ se lagāyā hai kabhī dast-e-ṣabā ko,
Ḍālī haiṅ kabhī gardan-e-mahtāb meṅ bāheṅ.

---

Chāhā hai isī raṅg meṅ lailā-e-waṭan ko,
Taṛpā hai isī ṭaur se dil uskī lagan meṅ,
Ḍhūṅḍī hai yūṅ-hī shauq-ne āsā'ish-e-manzil
Rukhsār ke kham meṅ, kabhī kākul kī shikan meṅ;

اُس جانِ جہاں کو بھی یُونہی قلب و نظر نے
ہنس ہنس کے صدا دِی، کبھی رو رو کے پُکارا
پُورے کیے سب حرفِ تمنّا کے تقاضے
ہر درد کو اُجیالا، ہر اِک غم کو سنوارا
واپس نہیں پھیرا کوئی فرمان جنُوں کا
تنہا نہیں لَوٹی کبھی آواز جرس کی
خیریّتِ جاں، راحتِ تن، صحّتِ داماں
سب بھُول گئیں مصلحتیں اہلِ ہوس کی

To that sweetheart too
Soul and flesh, every fibre,
Have called out with laughter,
Cried out with tears;
No longing of hers,
No summons unanswered,
Her griefs all transmuted,
Her sufferings made light;

Never devotion's
Prompting unheeded,
Never the trumpet
Left to ring hollowly—
Ease and indulgence,
Worldly distinction,
All the shrewd huckster's
Counsels forgotten.

*In the same way to that sweetheart of the world my heart and eyes*
*Laughingly called, sometimes weepingly cried out.*
*All the demands of her words of longing I fulfilled,*
*I made bright each pain, assuaged every grief;*
*No bidding of ecstasy was ever rejected,*
*Never did the sound of the bell return alone;*
*Welfare in life, comfort of body, correctness of costume (respectability),*
*All the advice of the people of ambition, were forgotten.*

Us jān-e-jahāṅ ko bhī yūṅ-hī qalb-o-naẓar-ne
Haṅs-haṅske ṣadā dī, kabhī ro-roke pukārā.
Pūre ki'e sab ḥarf-e-tamannā ke taqāẓe,
Har dard ko ujyālā, harĕk gham ko saṅwārā;
Wāpas nahīṅ pherā ko'ī farmān junūṅ kā,
Tanhā nahīṅ lauṭī kabhī āwāz jaras kī;
Khairīyat-e-jāṅ, rāḥat-e-tan, ṣĕḥḥat-e-dāmāṅ,
Sab bhūl-ga'īṅ maṣlaḥateṅ ahl-e-havas kī.

اس راہ میں جو سب پہ گزرتی ہے وہ گزری
تنہا پسِ زِنداں، کبھی رُسوا سرِبازار
گرجے ہیں بہت شیخ سرِ گوشۂ منبر
کڑکے ہیں بہت اہلِ حُکم برسرِ دربار
چھوڑا نہیں غیروں نے کوئی ناوکِ دُشنام
چھوٹی نہیں اپنوں سے کوئی طرزِ ملامت
اِس عشق، نہ اُس عشق پہ نادِم ہے مگر دِل
ہر داغ ہے اِس دِل میں بجز داغِ ندامت

What others on that road
Meet, I have met with:
Prison-cell solitude,
Marketplace calumny,
Priestly anathemas
Thundered from pulpits,
Threats and revilings
From places of power,

No barbed dart of insult
By strangers omitted,
No mode of upbraiding
By near and dear spared.
—My heart neither this love
Nor that love repents;
My heart that bears every
Scar, but of shame.

*What befalls everyone on that road befell me,*
*Solitary within the prison, sometimes dishonoured in the market-place;*
*The divines thundered a great deal from the pulpit corner,*
*The men of authority roared a great deal in the audience-chamber,*
*Strangers spared no arrow of calumny,*
*No manner of reproach was left out by my own folk.*
*But my heart feels shame neither for this love nor for that love;*
*There is every scar on this heart except the scar of shame.*

Is rāh meṅ jo sab pĕ guzartī hai vo guzrī,
Tanhā pas-e-zindāṅ, kabhī ruswā sar-e-bāzār;
Garje haiṅ bahut shaikh sar-e-gosha-e-miṅbar,
Kaṛke haiṅ bahut ahl-e-ḥukm bar sar-e-darbār.
Chhoṛā nahīṅ ghairoṅ-ne ko'ī nāvak-e-dushnām,
Chhūṭī nahīṅ apnoṅ se ko'ī t̤arz-e-malāmat.
Is 'ishq na us 'ishq pĕ nādim hai magar dil;
Har dāgh hai is dil meṅ bajuz dāgh-e-nadāmat.

# اُن طَلَبہ کے نام

## جو امن اور آزادی کی جِدّ و جَہد میں کام آئے

یہ کَون سخی ہَیں
جِن کے لہُو کی
اشرفیاں، چھَن چھَن، چھَن چھَن
دھرتی کے پیہم پیاسے
کشکول میں ڈھلتی جاتی ہیں
کشکول کو بھرتی جاتی ہیں
یہ کَون جواں ہیں ارضِ وطن
یہ لکھ لُٹ

## 30. TO SOME FOREIGN STUDENTS

*who gave their lives for peace and freedom*

Who are they, these
Free givers whose blood-drops,
Jingling coins, go pouring
Into earth's ever-thirsty
Begging-bowl, pour and run,
Filling the bowl brim-full?
What are they, land of their birth, these young
Self-squanderers whose

### *TO THOSE STUDENTS*

*who perished in the struggle for peace and freedom*

*Who are these generous ones,*
*Of whose blood*
*The gold coins, clink, clink,*
*Into the earth's continually thirsty*
*Begging-bowl are running,*
*Are filling up the begging-bowl?*
*Who are these young men, oh native land (of theirs),*
*These spendthrifts*

### UN ṬALABA KE NĀM

jo aman aur āzādī kī jidd-o-jahd meṅ kām ā'e

Ye kaun sak͟hī haiṅ
Jin-ke lahū kī
Ashrafyāṅ, chhan-chhan, chhan-chhan,
Dhartī ke paiham pyāse
Kashkol meṅ ḍhaltī-jātī haiṅ,
Kashkol ko bhartī-jātī haiṅ?
Ye kaun jawāṅ haiṅ, arẓ-e-waṭan,
Ye lakhluṭ

جن کے چشموں کی

بھرپور جوانی کا کُندن

یُوں خاک میں ریزہ ریزہ ہے

یوں کُوچہ کُوچہ بکھرا ہے

اے ارض وطن، اے ارض وطن

کیوں نوچ کے ہنس ہنس پھینک دِئے

اِن آنکھوں نے اپنے نیلم

اِن ہونٹوں نے اپنے مرجاں

اِن ہاتوں کی بے کل چاندی

کِس کام آئی؟ کِس ہات لگی؟


اے پُوچھنے والے پردیسی!

یہ طفل و جواں

Limbs' golden store
Of surging youth
Lies here in the dust, shattered—
Lies strewn about street and alley?
Oh land of their birth, oh land of their birth!
How could those eyes that laughed tear out
And toss their sapphire gems away,
Those lips their coral?
Who gained, who turned to profit,
Those hands' quivering silver?

Oh questioning stranger—
These striplings, these young lives,

*Of whose bodies*
*The brimming youth's pure gold*
*Is thus in fragments in the dust,*
*Is thus scattered street by street,*
*Oh (their) native land, oh native land?*
*Why did they tear out, laughing, and throw away,*
*These eyes their sapphires,*
*These lips their coral?*
*The restless silver of these hands,*
*To what use did it come, into whose possession did it fall?*

*Oh questioning foreigner,*
*These boys and youths*

Jin-ke jismoṅ kī
Bharpūr jawānī kā kundan
Yūṅ k͟hāk meṅ reza reza hai,
Yūṅ kūcha kūcha bikhrā hai,
Ai arẓ-e-waṭan, ai arẓ-e-waṭan?
Kyūṅ nochke haṅs-haṅs phaiṅk-di'e
In āṅkhoṅ-ne apne nīlam,
In hoṅṭoṅ-ne apne marjāṅ?
In hāṭon kī be-kal chāṅdī
Kis kām ā'ī? kis hāt lagī?

Ai pūchhne-wāle pardesī!
Ye ṭifl o jawāṅ

اُس نُور کے نَو رس موتی ہَیں
اُس آگ کی کچّی کلیاں ہَیں
جِس میٹھے نُور اور کڑوی آگ
سے ظُلم کی اندھی رات میں پھُوٹا
صُبحِ بغاوت کا گُلشن
اَور صُبح ہُوئی من من، تن تن
اِن جِسموں کا چاندی سونا
اِن چہروں کے نیلم مرجاں
جگ مگ جگ مگ، رخشاں رخشاں
جو دیکھنا چاہے پردیسی
پاس آئے دیکھے جی بھر کر
یہ زیست کی رانی کا جھُومر
یہ امن کی دیوی کا کنگن

Are fresh-grown pearls of that light,
New-budded shoots of that flame,
Soft light and devouring flame,
From which amid tyranny's dense night sprang
The rosebed dawn of revolt,
And dawn was in every nerve and soul.
Their argent and golden flesh,
Those coral and sapphire faces
That gleam and shine there and gleam—
Let the stranger who would see
Stand close, gaze long!
They are the jewelry of the queen of life,
They are the diadem of the goddess of peace.

*Are fresh pearls of that light,*
*Are new-grown buds of that fire,*
*From which sweet light and hot fire*
*In the dark night of tyranny there burst forth*
*The garden of the dawn of rebellion,*
*And there was dawn in every mind and body.*
*The silver and gold of these bodies,*
*The sapphire and coral of these faces,*
*Glittering, glittering, shining, shining—*
*The foreigner who wishes to see,*
*Let him come close and look his fill:*
*These are the ornament of the queen of life,*
*These are the bracelet of the goddess of peace.*

Us nūr ke nauras motī haiṅ,
Us āg kī kachchī kalyāṅ haiṅ,
Jis mīṭhe nūr aur kaṛvī āg
Se ẕulm kī āṅdhī rāt meṅ phūṭā
Ṣubḥ-e-ba<u>gh</u>āwat kā gulshan,
Aur ṣubḥ hū'ī man man, tan tan.
In jismoṅ kā chāṅdī sonā,
In chĕhroṅ ke nīlam marjāṅ,
Jag-mag jag-mag, ra<u>kh</u>shāṅ ra<u>kh</u>shāṅ,
Jo dekhnā chāhe pardesī
Pās ā'e dekhe jī bharkar:
Ye zīst kī rānī kā jhūmar,
Ye amn kī devī kā kaṅgan.

# اگست ۱۹۵۲

روشن کہیں بہار کے امکاں ہوئے تو ہیں
گلشن میں چاک چند گریباں ہوئے تو ہیں

اب بھی خزاں کا راج ہے لیکن کہیں کہیں
گوشے رہِ چمن میں غزل خواں ہوئے تو ہیں

ٹھہری ہوئی ہے شب کی سیاہی وہیں مگر
کچھ کچھ سحر کے رنگ پر افشاں ہوئے تو ہیں

## 31. AUGUST 1952

At last half-promise of a spring has come—
Some flowers tear open their green cloaks and bloom,

And here and there some garden nooks begin
Their warblings, and defy the wintry gloom.

Night's shadows hold their ground, but some faint streaks
Of day show, spreading each a rosy plume;

## *AUGUST 1952*

*Evident at last have become possibilities of spring,*
*In the flower-garden a few mantles have been torn;*
*It is still the reign of autumn, but here and there*
*Corners in the garden path have become song-uttering.*
*Night's darkness has remained in the same place, but*
*A few colours of morning have become feather-scattering.*

## AUGUST 1952

Raushan kahīṅ bahār ke imkāṅ hū'e to haiṅ,
Gulshan meṅ chāk chaṅd girībāṅ hū'e to haiṅ;
Ab bhī khazāṅ kā rāj hai, lekin kahīṅ kahīṅ
Goshe rah-e-chaman meṅ ghazal-khẉān hū'e to haiṅ.
Ṭhahrī hū'ī hai shab kī siyāhī wahīṅ, magar
Kuchh kuchh saḥar ke raṅg par-afshāṅ hū'e to haiṅ.

اِن میں لہُو جلا ہو ہمارا، کہ جان و دِل
محفِل میں کچھ چراغ فروزاں ہُوئے تو ہیں

ہاں کج کرو کُلاہ کہ سب کچھ لُٹا کے ہم
اب بے نیازِ گردشِ دوراں ہُوئے تو ہیں

اہلِ قفس کی صُبحِ چمن میں کھُلے گی آنکھ
بادِ صبا سے وعدہ و پیماں ہُوئے تو ہیں

ہے دشت اب بھی دشت، مگر خُونِ پا سے فیضؔ
سیراب چند خارِ مُغیلاں ہُوئے تو ہیں

And in the gathering, even if our own blood
Or breath must feed them, a few lamps light the room.

Tilt your proud cap! for we, the world well lost,
Never need fear what comes from Heaven's grand loom.

Caged eyes will open when dawn fills the garden:
Dawn's breeze they have had pledge and promise from.

Desert still desert, Faiz—but bleeding feet
Have saved some thorns at least from its dry tomb.


*Though in them our blood be burned, or our life and heart,*
*In the assembly some lamps have been lighted.*
*Yes, tilt your cap, for we, having thrown away everything,*
10  *Now have become independent of the time's revolutions.*
*The caged race's eye will open in the garden morning,*
*With the morning breeze there have been promise and pledge.*
*Desert is even now desert, but with the blood of the feet, Faiz,*
*Some mimosa-thorns have been watered.*


Maḥfil meṅ kuchh charāg̲h̲ furozāṅ hū'e to haiṅ.
Hāṅ kaj karo kulāh kĕ sab kuchh luṭāke ham
10  Ab be-nayāz-e-gardish-e-daurāṅ hū'e to haiṅ.
Ahl-e-qafas kī ṣubḥ-e-chaman meṅ khulegī āṅkh,
Bād-e-ṣabā se va'da-o-paimāṅ hū'e to haiṅ.
Hai dasht ab bhī dasht, magar k̲h̲ūn-e-pā se, Faiz,
Serāb chaṅd k̲h̲ār-e-mug̲h̲īlāṅ hū'e to haiṅ.

# نثار میں تری گلیوں کے....

نثار میں تری گلیوں کے اے وطن کہ جہاں
چلی ہے رسم کہ کوئی نہ سر اُٹھا کے چلے
جو کوئی چاہنے والا طواف کو نکلے
نظر چُرا کے چلے، جسم و جاں بچا کے چلے

ہے اہلِ دل کے لئے اب یہ نظمِ بست و کُشاد
کہ سنگ و خشت مُقیّد ہیں اور سگ آزاد

## 32. BURY ME UNDER YOUR PAVEMENTS

Bury me, oh my country, under your pavements,
Where no man now dare walk with head held high,
Where your true lovers bringing you their homage
Must go in furtive fear of life or limb;
For new-style law and order are in use,
Good men learn,—'Stones locked up, and dogs turned loose'.

### *MAY I BE A SACRIFICE TO YOUR STREETS*

*May I be a sacrifice to your streets, oh fatherland, where*
*It has become custom that no-one shall go with head lifted,*
*And that any lover who comes out on pilgrimage*
*Must go with furtive looks, go in fear of body and life;*
*Applied to the people of heart now there is this method of administration,*
*That stones and bricks are locked up, and dogs free.*

### NIS̤ĀR MAIN TĔRĪ GALYOṄ KE

Nis̤ār maiṅ tĕrī galyoṅ ke, ai waṭan, kĕ jahāṅ
Chalī hai rasm kĕ ko'ī na sar uṭhāke chale,
Jo ko'ī chāhne-wālā t̤awāf ko nikle
Naẓar churāke chale, jism-o-jāṅ bachāke chale;
Hai ahl-i-dil ke liye ab ye naẓm-e-bast-o-kushād,
Kĕ saṅg o k͟h͟isht muqaiyad haiṅ aur sag āzād.

بہت ہے ظُلم کے دستِ بہانہ جُو کے لئے
جو چند اہلِ جُنوں تیرے نام لیوا ہَیں
بنے ہَیں اہلِ ہَوَس مُدّعی بھی مُنصِف بھی
کِسے وکیل کریں، کِس سے مُنصِفی چاہیں

مگر گُذارنے والوں کے دِن گُذرتے ہَیں
ترے فِراق میں یُوں صُبح و شام کرتے ہَیں
بُجھا جو روزنِ زِنداں تو دِل یہ سمجھا ہے
کہ تیری مانگ سِتاروں سے بھر گئی ہو گی
چمک اُٹھے ہَیں سلاسِل تو ہم نے جانا ہے
کہ اب سحر ترے رُخ پر بکھر گئی ہو گی
غرض تصوّرِ شام و سحر میں جیتے ہَیں
گرفتِ سایۂ دِیوار و در میں جیتے ہَیں

Your name still cried by a rash zealot few
Inflames the itching hand of tyranny;
Villains are judges and usurpers both—
Who is our advocate, where shall we seek justice?
But all hours man must spend are somehow spent;
How do we pass these days of banishment?

When my cell's window-slit grows dim, I seem
To see your hair spangled with starry tinsel;
When chains grow once more visible, I think
I see your face sprinkled with dawn's first rays;
In fantasies of the changing hours we live,
Held fast by shadowy gates and towers we live.

*It is enough for tyranny's pretext-seeking hand*
*If a few enthusiasts call on your name;*
*The men of ambition have become both prosecutor and judge:*
*Whom are we to make our advocate, from whom are we to desire justice?*
*But the days of those who are to pass them do pass;*
*In separation from you they spend their mornings-and-evenings thus.*
*When the prison grating has grown dark, my heart has believed*
*That your hair-parting must have been filled with stars;*
*When the chains have shone out, I have thought*
*That now daybreak must have been scattered over your face.*
*In short I live in fancies of evening and morning,*
*I live in the grasp of the shadow of wall and gate.*

Bahut hai ẓulm ke dast-e-bahāna-jū ke liye
Jo chand ahl-e-junūṅ tere nām-levā haiṅ;
Bane haiṅ ahl-e-havas mudda'ī bhī, munṣif bhī:
Kise vakīl kareṅ, kis-se munṣifī chāheṅ?
Magar guzārne-wāloṅ ke din guzarte haiṅ,
Tĕre firāq meṅ yūṅ ṣubḥ-o-shām karte haiṅ.
Bujhā jo rauzan-e-zindāṅ to dil ye samjhā hai
Kĕ terī māṅg sitāroṅ se bhar-ga'ī hogī;
Chamak-uṭhe haiṅ salāsil to ham-ne jānā hai
Kĕ ab saḥar tĕre rukh par bikhar-ga'ī hogī.
Gharaẓ taṣawwur-e-shām-o-saḥar meṅ jīte haiṅ,
Girift-e-sāya-e-dīwār-o-dar meṅ jīte haiṅ.

یُونہی ہمیشہ اُلجھتی رہی ہَے ظُلم سے خلق
نہ اُن کی رسم نئی ہَے، نہ اپنی ریت نئی
یُونہی ہمیشہ کھلائے ہیں ہم نے آگ میں پھُول
نہ اُن کی ہار نئی ہَے نہ اپنی جیت نئی

اِسی سبب سے فلک کا گِلا نہیں کرتے
ترے فِراق میں ہم دِل بُرا نہیں کرتے
گر آج تجُھ سے جُدا ہیں تو کل بہم ہوں گے
یہ رات بھر کی جُدائی تو کوئی بات نہیں
گر آج اَوج پہ ہَے طالعِ رقیب تو کیا
یہ چار دِن کی خُدائی تو کوئی بات نہیں
جو تجُھ سے عہدِ وفا اُستوار رکھتے ہَیں
علاجِ گردِشِ لَیل و نہار رکھتے ہَیں

This war is old of tyrants and mankind:
Their ways not new, nor ours; the fires they kindle
To scorch us, age by age we turn to flowers;
Not new our triumph, not new their defeat.
Against fate therefore we make no complaint,
Our hearts though exiled from you do not faint.

Parted today, tomorrow we shall meet—
And what is one short night of separation?
Today our enemies' star is at its zenith—
But what is their brief week of playing God?
Those who keep firm their vows to you are proof
Against the whirling hours, time's warp and woof.

*In this same way tyranny and mankind have always been at odds:*
*Their (the tyrants') ways are not new, nor is our fashion new;*
*In this same way we have always made flowers blossom in the fire;*
*Their defeat is not new, nor is our victory new.*
*For this reason I do not make complaint against my fate,*
*In separation from you I do not let my heart sink.*
*If today I am separated from you, tomorrow we shall be together,*
*This separation of one night is nothing;*
*If today the rival's fortune is at the summit, what of it?*
*This godhood of four days is nothing.*
*Those who keep firm their vow of fidelity to you*
*Possess the remedy against the revolutions of night and day.*

Yūṅ-hī hamesha ulajhtī-rahī hai z̤ulm se k͟halq,
Na unkī rasm na'ī hai, na apnī rīt na'ī;
Yūṅ-hī hamesha khilā'e haiṅ ham-ne āg meṅ phūl,
Na unkī hār na'ī hai, na apnī jīt na'ī.
Isī sabab se falak kā gilā nahīṅ karte,
Tĕre firāq meṅ ham dil burā nahīṅ karte.
Gar āj tujh-se judā haiṅ to kal baham hoṅge,
Ye rāt bhar kī judā'ī to ko'ī bāt nahīṅ;
Gar āj auj pĕ hai t̤āli'-e-raqīb to kyā,
Ye chār din kī k͟hudā'ī to ko'ī bāt nahīṅ.
Jo tujh-se 'ahd-e-wafā ustuwār rakhte haiṅ
'ilāj-e-gardish-e-lail-o-nahār rakhte haiṅ.

# زنداں کی ایک شام

شام کے پیچ و خم ستاروں سے
زینہ زینہ اُتر رہی ہے رات
یوں صبا پاس سے گزُرتی ہے
جیسے کہہ دی کسی نے پیار کی بات
صحنِ زنداں کے بے وطن اشجار
سرنگوں، محو ہیں بنانے میں
دامنِ آسماں پہ نقش و نگار
شانۂ بام پر دمکتا ہے
مہرباں چاندنی کا دستِ جمیل

## 33. A PRISON NIGHTFALL

Step by step by its twisted stairway
Of constellations, night descends;
Close, as close as a voice that whispers
Tendernesses, a breeze drifts by;
Trees of the prison courtyard, exiles
With drooping head, are lost in broidering
Arabesques on the skirt of heaven.

Graciously on that roof's high crest
The moonlight's exquisite fingers gleam;

### *A PRISON EVENING*

*By evening's devious stars*
*Rung by rung night is coming down;*
*A breeze passes close by,*
*As if someone has spoken a word of love;*
*In the prison yard trees, with no native land,*
*Head drooping, are absorbed in making*
*On the skirt of heaven images and pictures;*
*On the crest of the roof is glittering*
*The beautiful hand of the gracious moonlight;*

### ZINDĀṄ KĪ EK SHĀM

Shām ke pech-o-kham sitāroṅ se
Zīna zīna utar-rahī hai rāt;
Yūṅ ṣabā pās se guzartī hai
Jaise kah-dī kisī-ne pyār kī bāt;
Ṣaḥn-e-zindāṅ ke be-waṭan ashjār
Sar-nigūṅ maḥv haiṅ banāne meṅ
Dāman-e-āsmāṅ pĕ naqsh-o-nigār;
Shāna-e-bām par damaktā hai
Mĕhrbāṅ chāṅdnī kā dast-e-jamīl;

خاک میں گھل گئی ہے آبِ نجوم

نُور میں گھل گیا ہے عرش کا نیل

سبز گوشوں میں نیلگوں سائے

لہلہاتے ہیں جس طرح دل میں

موجِ دردِ فراقِ یار آئے


دل سے پیہم خیال کہتا ہے

اتنی شیریں ہے زندگی اس پل

ظلم کا زہر گھولنے والے

کامراں ہو سکیں گے آج نہ کل

جلوہ گاہِ وصال کی شمعیں

وہ بُجھا بھی چُکے اگر تو کیا

چاند کو گُل کریں تو ہم جانیں

Star-lustre swallowed into the dust,
Sky-azure blanched into one white glow,
Green nooks filling with deep-blue shadows,
Waveringly, like separation's
Bitterness eddying into the mind.

One thought keeps running in my heart—
Such nectar life is at this instant,
Those who mix the tyrants' poisons
Can never, now or tomorrow, win.
What if they put the candles out
That light love's throneroom? let them put out
The moon, then we shall know their power.

*The sheen of the stars has dissolved into the dust,*
*The blue of the sky has dissolved into light,*
*In green corners dark-blue shadows*
*Waver, as if into the heart*
*A ripple of pain for separation from the loved one were coming.*

*A thought continually says to my heart:*
*Life is so sweet this moment,*
*The mixers of tyranny's poison*
*Will not be able to be successful today nor tomorrow.*
*The lamps of the bridal-chamber of union,*
*Even if they have put them out, what then?*
*Were they to extinguish the moon, then we should acknowledge them.*

K͟hāk meṅ ghul-ga'ī hai āb-e-najūm,
Nūr meṅ ghul-gayā hai 'arsh kā nīl,
Sabz goshoṅ meṅ nīlgūṅ sā'e
Lahlahāte haiṅ, jis ṭaraḥ dil meṅ
Mauj-e-dard-e-firāq-e-yār ā'e.

Dil se paiham k͟hayāl kahtā hai
Itnī shīrīṅ hai zindagī is pal
Ẓulm kā zahr gholne-wāle
Kāmrāṅ ho-sakeṅge āj na kal.
Jalwagāh-e-viṣāl kī sham'eṅ
Vo bujhā bhī chuke agar, to kyā?
Chāṅd ko gul kareṅ to ham jāneṅ.

# زِنداں کی ایک صُبح

رات باقی تھی ابھی جب سرِ بالیں آکر
چاند نے مُجھ سے کہا "جاگ! سحر آئی ہَے
جاگ! اِس شب جو مَے خواب تِرا حصّہ تھی
جام کے لب سے تہِ جام اُتر آئی ہَے"
عکسِ جاناں کو وِدع کرکے اُٹھی میری نظر
شب کے ٹھہرے ہُوئے پانی کی سیَہ چادر پر
جا بجا رقص میں آنے لگے چاندی کے بھنور
چاند کے ہاتھ سے تاروں کے کنول گِر گِر کر
ڈوبتے، تَیرتے، مُرجھاتے رہے، کھلتے رہے
رات اَور صُبح بہُت دیر گلے مِلتے رہے

## 34. A PRISON DAYBREAK

It was still dark, when standing by my pillow
The moon said to me 'Waken, dawn is here:
The share poured for you of this night's wine of sleep
Has sunk from brim to bottom of the cup.'
—I took farewell of my love's image, and gazed
Out over the dim coverlet of the night's
Slow-ebbing flood, where here and there a dance
Of argent ripples flickered, while the stars,
Like lotus-petals fallen from the moon's hand,
Came sinking, floating, fading, opening out;
Daybreak and night lay long in each other's arms.

### *A PRISON DAYBREAK*

*There was night still remaining when coming beside my pillow*
*The moon said to me 'Waken, morning has come;*
*Waken! the wine of sleep that was your portion this night*
*Has sunk from the lip of the cup to the bottom of the cup.'*
*Taking leave of the image of my sweetheart I lifted my glance*
*To the black coverlet of the night's lingering flood:*
*Here and there whirlpools of silver began to come in a dance;*
*From the moon's hand lotuses of stars falling, falling,*
*Sinking, swimming, kept fading, kept opening;*
*Night and dawn for a long time were embracing.*

### ZINDĀN KĪ EK ṢUBḤ

Rāt bāqī thī abhī jab sar-e-bālīṅ ākar
Chāṅd-ne mujh-se kahā 'Jāg! saḥar ā'ī hai;
Jāg! is shab jo mai-e-k͟hẉāb tĕrā hiṣṣa thī
Jām ke lab se tah-e-jām utar-ā'ī hai.'
'aks-e-jānāṅ ko vida' karke uṭhī merī naz̤ar
Shab ke ṭhahre hū'e pānī kī siya chādar par:
Jā-ba-jā raqṣ meṅ āne-lage chāṅdī ke bhaṅwar;
Chāṅd ke hāth se tāroṅ ke kaṅval gir-girkar
Ḍūbte, tairte, murjhāte-rahe, khilte-rahe,
Rāt aur ṣubḥ bahut der gale milte-rahe.

صحنِ زنداں میں رفیقوں کے سنہرے چہرے
سطحِ ظلمت سے دمکتے ہوئے ابھرے کم کم
نیند کی اوس نے اُن چہروں سے دھو ڈالا تھا
دیس کا درد، فراقِ رُخِ محبوب کا غم
دُور نوبت ہوئی، پھرنے لگے بیزار قدم
زرد، فاقوں کے ستائے ہوئے پہرے والے
اہلِ زنداں کے غضبناک، خروشاں نالے
جن کی باہوں میں پھرا کرتے ہیں باہیں ڈالے
لذّتِ خواب سے مخمور ہوائیں جاگیں
جیل کی زہر بھری چوُر، صدائیں جاگیں

Golden in the jail yard my comrades' features
Slowly emerging, a glow against the darkness,
Washed clean by oblivion's dews of brooding grief
For loved face lost, or care for native land;—
A far-off drum sounding, a shuffle of feet
Of pallid famished guards starting their rounds,
And arm in arm and on and on with them
The angry din of prisoner and complaint.
Light winds still drunk with dream-delights are stirring;
With them, ghostly, a prison's bodeful noises:

*In the prison yard the golden faces of comrades,*
*Shining out from the surface of darkness, grew little by little;*
*The dew of sleep had washed away from those faces*
*Grief for country, pain of separation from the face of the beloved.*
*Far off there has been a drum, feeble steps have begun to move about;*
*Yellow, oppressed with hunger, the sentinels—*
*With whom the frightful, resounding laments of the people of the prison*
*Arm in arm keep moving about.*
*Breezes drunk with the pleasure of sleep have awakened,*
*The jail's poison-filled, broken sounds have awakened:*

Ṣaḥn-e-zindāṅ meṅ rafīqoṅ ke sunahre chĕhre
Saṭ'ḥ-e-ẓulmat se damakte hū'e ubhre kam kam;
Nīṅd kī os-ne un chĕhroṅ se dho-ḍālā thā
Des kā dard, firāq-e-rukh-e-maḥbūb kā gham.
Dūr naubat hū'ī, phirne-lage bezār qadam,
Zard, fāqoṅ ke satā'e hū'e pahre-wāle:
Ahl-e-zindāṅ ke ghaẓabnāk, kharoshāṅ nāle
Jin-kī bāhoṅ meṅ phirā-karte haiṅ bāheṅ ḍāle.
Lazzat-e-khwāb se makhmūr hawā'eṅ jāgīṅ,
Jel kī zahr-bharī, chūr, ṣadā'eṅ jāgīṅ.

دُور دروازہ کھلا کوئی، کوئی بند ہُوا
دُور مچلی کوئی زنجیر، مچل کے روئی
دُور اُترا کسی تالے کے جگر میں خنجر
سر پٹکنے لگا رہ رہ کے دریچہ کوئی
گویا پھر خواب سے بیدار ہُوئے دُشمنِ جاں
سنگ و فولاد سے ڈھالے ہُوئے جنّاتِ گراں
جن کے چنگل میں شب و روز ہیں فریاد کُناں
میرے بےکار شب و روز کی نازک پریاں
اپنے شہ پُور کی رہ دیکھ رہی ہیں یہ اسیر
جس کے ترکش میں ہیں اُمّید کے جلتے ہُوئے تیر

A distant door opens, another shuts,
A distant chain scrapes sullenly, scrapes and sobs,
Far off a dagger plunges in some lock's vitals,
A shutter rattles, rattles, beating its head.

My mortal foes have risen again from sleep,
Grim monsters welded out of stone and steel,
Fast in whose talons daylong and nightlong wail
Those gossamer spirits, my empty nights and days,
Captives watching and waiting for their prince
Whose quiver holds the burning arrows of hope.

*Far away some door has opened, some other has closed,*
*Far away some chain has grumbled, and after grumbling w*
*Far away a dagger has sunk into some lock's liver,*
*Some window has begun to bang its head again and again;–*
*As if the enemies of life have roused again from sleep,*
*Heavy demons cast from stone and steel,*
*In whose grasp are making lament night and day*
*The delicate fairies of my useless nights and days;*
*These prisoners are watching for their prince,*
*In whose quiver are hope's burning arrows.*

Dūr darwāza khulā ko'ī, ko'ī baṅd hū'ā,
Dūr machlī ko'ī zanjīr, machalke ro'ī,
Dūr utarā kisī tāle ke jigar meṅ khanjar,
Sar paṭakne-lagā rah-rahke darīcha ko'ī;—
Goyā phir khẉāb se bedār hū'e dushman-e-jāṅ,
Sang o faulād se ḍhāle hū'e jinnāt-e-girāṅ,
Jinke chuṅgal meṅ shab-o-roz haiṅ faryād-kunāṅ
Mere be-kār shab-o-roz kī nāzuk paryāṅ;
Apne shahpūr kī rāh dekh-rahī haiṅ ye asīr
Jiske tarkash meṅ haiṅ ummed ke jalte hū'e tīr.

# زِندان نامہ

# PRISON THOUGHTS

*PRISON THOUGHTS*

ZINDĀN-NĀMA

# اے روشنیوں کے شہر

سبزہ سبزہ سُوکھ رہی ہے پھیکی زرد دوپہر
دیواروں کو چاٹ رہا ہے تنہائی کا زہر
دُور اُفق تک گھٹتی، بڑھتی، اُٹھتی، گرتی رہتی ہے
کُہر کی صُورت بے رَونق دردوں کی گدلی لہر
بستا ہے اِس کُہر کے پیچھے روشنیوں کا شہر

اَے رَوشنیوں کے شہر

کَون کہے کِس سمت ہَے تیری رَوشنیوں کی راہ
ہر جانب بے نُور کھڑی ہَے ہجر کی شہر پناہ
تھک کر ہر سُو بیٹھ رہی ہَے شوق کی ماند سپاہ

## 35. OH CITY OF MANY LIGHTS

Listless and wan, green patch by patch, noonday dries up;
Pale solitude with venomed tongue licks at these walls;
Far as the skyline, like a fog, an oozy tide
Of blockish misery swells and shrinks, heaves up and falls.

Beyond that fog the lights of my thronged city lie.
    Oh city of many lights!—
Who could make out what way from here your lights
    are? Dark
As a town's ramparts isolation hems me in,
And war-worn hope's faint soldiery droops on every side.

### *OH CITY OF LIGHTS*

*Greenery by greenery, the pallid yellow noon is withering,*
*The poison of solitude is licking the walls;*
*Far away to the horizon keeps dwindling, swelling, rising, sinking,*
*Like a mist, the turbid wave of unlovely pains.*
*Behind this mist the city of lights is situated;*
*Oh city of lights;*
*Who could say in what direction is the road to your lights?*
*On every side stand the unlit city-walls of banishment:*
*Weary, in every direction, the exhausted army of ardour is sitting.*

### AI RAUSHNIYOṄ KE SHAHR

Sabza sabza sūkh-rahī hai phīkī zard do-pahr,
Dīwāroṅ ko chāṭ-rahā hai tanhā'ī kā zahr;
Dūr ufaq tak ghaṭṭī, baṛhtī, uṭhtī, girtī-rahtī hai
Kuhr kī ṣūrat be-raunaq dardoṅ kī gadlī lahr.
Bastā hai is kuhr ke pīchhe raushniyoṅ kā shahr;
Ai raushniyoṅ ke shahr,
Kaun kahe kis simt hai terī raushniyoṅ kī rāh?
Har jānib be-nūr khaṛī hai hijr kī shahr-panāh:
Thakkar har sū baiṭh-rahī hai shauq kī māṅd sipāh.

آج مرا دِل فکر میں ہے

اے روشنیوں کے شہر

شب خوں سے مُنہ پھیر نہ جائے ارمانوں کی رَو

خَیر ہو تیری لیلاؤں کی، اِن سب سے کہہ دو

آج کی شب جب دِیئے جلائیں اُونچی رکھّیں لَو

Today doubt fills my soul.
Oh city of many lights,
Let hope's armed ranks not turn from their night-marching yet!
Fortune befriend your loving hearts; say to them all—
This evening, when the lamps are lit, turn the wick high.

*Today my heart is in anxiety;*
*Oh city of lights,*
*May the torrent of aspirations not turn its face away from the night-attack!*
*May it be well with your sweethearts; say to them all,*
*This evening when they light the lamps let them turn the flame high.*

Āj mĕrā dil fikr meṅ hai;
Ai raushniyoṅ ke shahr,
Shabkhūṅ se muṅh pher na jā'e armānoṅ kī rau.
Khair ho terī lailāọṅ kī, in sab se kah-do
Āj kī shab jab diye jalā'en ūṅchī rakkheṅ lau.

# دریچہ

گڑی ہیں کتنی صلیبیں مرے دریچے میں
ہر ایک اپنے مسیحا کے خوں کا رنگ لیے
ہر ایک وصلِ خداوند کی امنگ لیے

کسی پہ کرتے ہیں ابرِ بہار کو قرباں
کسی پہ قتل مہِ تابناک کرتے ہیں
کسی پہ ہوتی ہے سرمست شاخسار دونیم
کسی پہ بادِ صبا کو ہلاک کرتے ہیں

## 36. THE WINDOW

In my barred window is hung many a cross,
Each coloured with the blood of its own Christ,
Each craving to hug tight a divine form.

On one the heaven's spring cloud is sacrificed,
On one the radiant moon is crucified,
On one is torn asunder the trance-filled grove,
And on another the delicate breeze has died.

### *THE WINDOW*

*In my window how many crosses are fixed,*
*Each with the colour of the blood of its Messiah,*
*Each with the hope of union with its Lord.*
*On one they make sacrifice of the spring cloud,*
*On one they murder the bright moon,*
*On one the rapt park is cut in two,*
*On one they put to death the morning breeze.*

### DARĪCHA

Gaṛtī haiṅ kitnī ṣalībeṅ mĕre darīche meṅ,
Harek apne masīḥā ke khūṅ kā raṅg liye,
Harek vaṣl-e-khudāwaṅd kī umaṅg liye.
Kisī pĕ karte haiṅ abr-e-bahār ko qurbāṅ,
Kisī pĕ qatl mah-e-tābnāk karte haiṅ,
Kisī pĕ hotī hai sarmast shākhsār do nīm,
Kisī pĕ bād-e-ṣabā ko halāk karte haiṅ.

ہر آئے دِن یہ خُداوندگانِ مہر و جمال
لہُو میں غرق مرے غم کدے میں آتے ہیں
اَور آئے دِن مری نظروں کے سامنے اُن کے
شہیدِ جسم سلامت اُٹھائے جاتے ہیں

Daily these kind and beautiful godlike things
Come weltering in their blood to my bitter cell;
And day by day before my watching eyes
Their martyred bodies are raised up and made well.

*Each day that comes these deities of kindness and beauty*
*Drowned in blood come into my house of grief,*
*And daily before my eyes their*
*Martyr-bodies are lifted up, healed.*

Har ā'e din ye khudāwańdgān-e-mehr-o-jamāl
Lahū meń gharq mĕre gham-kade meń āte haiń,
Aur ā'e din mĕrī nazroń ke sāmne unke
Shahīd jism salāmat uṭhā'e-jāte haiń.

# آجاؤ ایفرِیقا!

آ جاؤ، مَیں نے سُن لی ترِے ڈھول کی ترنگ
آجاؤ، مست ہوگئی میرے لہُو کی تال
"آ جاؤ ایفرِیقا"

آجاؤ، مَیں نے دُھول سے ماتھا اُٹھا لِیا
آجاؤ، مَیں نے چِھیل دی آنکھوں سے غم کی چھال
آجاؤ، مَیں نے درد سے بازُو چھُڑا لِیا
آجاؤ، مَیں نے نوچ دِیا بے کسی کا جال
"آجاؤ ایفرِیقا"

## 37. 'AFRICA, COME BACK'

I have caught the madness of your drum,
My wild blood beats and throbs with it—come,
    Africa, come!

Come, from the dust I have raised my head,
Torn misery's bandage from my face,
Wrenched my arm free from pain's grip, cut
My way through the web of helplessness—
    Africa, come!

### *'COME, AFRICA!'*

*Come, I have heard the ecstasy of your drum—*
*Come, the beating of my blood has become mad—*
*'Come, Africa!'*
*Come, I have lifted my forehead from the dust—*
*Come, I have scraped from my eyes the skin of grief—*
*Come, I have released my arm from pain—*
*Come, I have clawed through the snare of helplessness—*
*'Come, Africa!'*

### Ā-JĀO AĪFRĪQ̣Ā!

Ā-jāo, maiṅ-ne sun-lī tĕre ḍhol kī taraṅg,
Ā-jāo, mast ho-ga'ī mere lahū kī tāl—
'Ā-jāo, Aifrīqā!'
Ā-jāo, maiṅ-ne dhūl se māthā uṭhā-liyā,
Ā-jāo, maiṅ-ne chhīl-dī āṅkhoṅ se g̲h̲am kī chhāl,
Ā-jāo, maiṅ-ne dard se bāzū chhuṛā-liyā,
Ā-jāo, maiṅ-ne noch-diyā be-kasī kā jāl—
'Ā-jāo, Aifrīqā!'

پنجے میں ہتھکڑی کی کڑی بن گئی ہے گُرز
گردن کا طوق توڑ کے ڈھالی ہے مَیں نے ڈھال
"آجاؤ ایفریقا"
جلتے ہَیں ہر کچھار میں بھالوں کے مِرگ نَین
دُشمن لہُو سے رات کی کالک ہُوئی ہے لال
"آجاؤ ایفریقا"
دھرتی دھڑک رہی ہے مرے ساتھ ایفریقا
دریا تھرک رہا ہے تو بَن دے رہا ہے تال
مَیں ایفریقا ہُوں، دھار لیا مَیں نے تیرا رُوپ
مَیں تو ہُوں، میری چال ہے تیری ببر کی چال
"آجاؤ ایفریقا"
آؤ ببر کی چال
"آجاؤ ایفریقا"

The shattered manacle is my mace,
From the broken fetter I forge my shield—
Africa, come!
Spears burn like gazelles' eyes through the reeds,
With enemy blood night's shades turn red—
Africa, come!

The earth's heart, Africa, beats with mine,
The river dances, the woods keep time;
I am Africa, I put on your mask,
I am you, my step is your lion tread,
Africa—come,
Come with your lion-tread,
Africa, come!

*In my grasp a link of the manacle has become a mace,*
*I have broken the iron-collar on my neck and moulded it into a shield—*
*'Come, Africa!'*
*On every riverside burn the deer-eyes of spears,*
*With enemy blood the blackness of night has turned red,*
*'Come, Africa!'*
*The earth is throbbing along with me, Africa,*
*The river dances and the forest beats time;*
*I am Africa, I have taken your figure,*
*I am you, my walk is your lion walk:*
*'Come, Africa!'*
*Come with lion walk—*
*'Come, Africa!'*

Panje meṅ hathkaṛī kī kaṛī ban-ga'ī hai gurz,
Gardan kā ṭauq toṛke ḍhālī hai maiṅ-ne ḍhāl—
'Ā-jāo, Aifrīqā!'
Jalte haiṅ har kachhār meṅ bhāloṅ ke mirg-nain,
Dushman lahū se rāt kī kālak hū'ī hai lāl—
'Ā-jāo, Aifrīqā!'
Dhartī dhaṛak-rahī hai mĕre sāth, Aifrīqā,
Daryā thirak-rahā hai to ban de-rahā hai tāl;
Maiṅ Aifrīqā hūṅ, dhār-liyā maiṅ-ne terā rūp,
Maiṅ tū hūṅ, merī chāl hai terī babar kī chāl:
'Ā-jāo, Aifrīqā!'
Ao babar kī chāl—
'Ā-jāo, Aifrīqā!'

# یہ فصلِ اُمیدوں کی ہمدم

سب کاٹ دو
بِسمِل پودوں کو
بے آب سِسکتے مت چھوڑو
سب نوچ لو
بے کل پھولوں کو
شاخوں پہ بِلکتے مت چھوڑو
یہ فصل اُمیدوں کی ہمدم
اِس بار بھی غارت جائے گی
سب مِحنت صُبحوں شاموں کی
اب کے بھی اکارت جائے گی

## 38. THIS HARVEST OF HOPES

Cut them all down, these crippled plants,
Not leave them to their last parched distress!
Tear off from the spray these twisted blooms,
Not leave them to hang in wretchedness!

This harvest of smiling hopes, my friend,
Is doomed to be blighted once again:
Those labours that fill your days and nights
Are doomed to be this time too in vain.

### *THIS HARVEST OF HOPES, COMPANION*

*Cut down all*
*The wounded plants,*
*Do not leave them without water, at their last gasp;*
*Tear away all*
*The writhing flowers,*
*Do not leave them pining on the boughs.*
*This harvest of hopes, companion,*
*This time too will go to ruin,*
*All the toil of mornings and evenings*
*Now too will prove worthless.*

### YE FAṢL UMEDOṄ KĪ, HAMDAM

Sab kāṭ-do
Bismil paudoṅ ko,
Be-āb sisakte mat chhoṛo;
Sab noch-lo
Be-kal phūloṅ ko,
Shā<u>kh</u>oṅ pĕ bilakte mat chhoṛo.
Ye faṣl umedoṅ kī, hamdam,
Is bār bhī <u>gh</u>ārat jā'egī,
Sab mĕḥnat ṣubḥoṅ shāmoṅ kī
Abke bhī akārat jā'egī.

کھیتی کے کونوں کھدروں میں
پھر اپنے لہو کی کھاد بھرو
پھر مٹّی سینچو اشکوں سے
پھر اگلی رُت کی فکر کرو
پھر اگلی رُت کی فکر کرو
جب پھر اِک بار اُجڑنا ہے
اِک فصل پکی تو بھر پایا
جب تک تو یہی کچھ کرنا ہے

But once more feed with your blood dry clods
In crannies and corners about the field,
Moisten them with your tears afresh,
Then think of the coming season's yield—

Yes, think of the coming season's yield,
When ruin will once more strike these lands. . . .
Some day a ripe harvest shall be ours;
Till that day, we must plough the sands.

*In holes and corners of the ploughland*
*Once more pour the fertiliser of your blood,*
*Once more water the earth with tears;*
*Once more take thought for the next season,*
*Once more take thought for the next season,*
*When once more it must come to ruin.*
*One harvest ripened, we shall have satisfaction,*
*Until which time we must go on doing the same thing.*

Khetī ke konoṅ-khudroṅ meṅ
Phir apne lahū kī khād bharo,
Phir miṭṭī sīṅcho ashkoṅ se;
Phir aglī rut kī fikr karo,
Phir aglī rut kī fikr karo,
Jab phir ĕk bār ujaṛnā hai.
Ĕk fasl pakī to bhar-pāyā,
Jab tak to yĕhī kuchh karnā hai.

# دستِ تہِ سنگ

DURESS

*'THE HAND UNDER THE ROCK*

DAST-E-TAH-E-SAṄG

# سنکیانگ

اب کوئی طبل بجے گا نہ کوئی شاہ سوار
صبح دم موت کی وادی کو روانہ ہوگا؛
اب کوئی جنگ نہ ہوگی نہ کبھی رات گئے
خون کی آگ کو اشکوں سے بجھانا ہوگا
کوئی دل دھڑکے گا شب بھر نہ کسی آنگن میں
وہم منحوس پرندے کی طرح آئے گا
سہم خوں خوار درندے کی طرح آئے گا۔
اب کوئی جنگ نہ ہوگی، مے و ساغر لاؤ
خوں لٹانا نہ کبھی اشک بہانا ہوگا۔
ساقیا! رقص کوئی رقصِ صبا کی صورت
مطربا! کوئی غزل رنگِ حنا کی صورت

## 39. SINKIANG

No more now shall the drum sound, and no more
The horseman ride at dawn towards death's ravine;
War never any more, no need of tears
At dead of night to quench the burning pain,
No heart to shudder through the dark, no courtyard
For terror like a ravening beast to enter,
Or boding, like a bird of evil omen.
War never any more!—bring wine, bring goblet—
No more the squandered blood or the rushing tear;
Saqi! a dance, like the dancing breeze of dawn—
Minstrel! a song, like the scarlet stain of henna.

### *SINKIANG*

*Now no drum shall play, nor shall any cavalier*
*Set off at daybreak to the valley of death;*
*Now there shall be no war, nor ever late at night*
*Will fire in the blood have to be quenched with tears.*
*No heart shall quiver all night, nor in any courtyard*
*Shall causeless-anxiety come like an ill-omened bird,*
*Shall fear come like a bloodthirsty beast of prey.*
*Now there shall be no war,—bring wine and wine-cup!*
*There will never have to be spilling blood nor shedding tear.*
*Cupbearer! some dance, like the dance of the morning breeze;*
*Minstrel! some song, like the colour of henna.*

### SINKYĀṄG

Ab ko'ī ṭabl bajegā na ko'ī shāhsawār
Ṣubḥ-dam maut kī wādī ko rawāna hogā;
Ab ko'ī jaṅg na hogī, na kabhī rāt ga'e
Khūn kī āg ko ashkoṅ se bujhānā hogā.
Ko'ī dil dhaṛkegā shab bhar na kisī āṅgan meṅ
Vahm manḥūs parinde kī ṭaraḥ ā'egā,
Sahm khūṅkhwār darinde kī ṭaraḥ ā'egā.
Ab ko'ī jaṅg na hogī, mai o sāghir lāo!
Khūṅ luṭānā na kabhī ashk bahānā hogā.
Sāqiyā! raqṣ ko'ī raqṣ-e-ṣabā kī ṣūrat;
Muṭribā! ko'ī ghazal raṅg-e-ḥinā kī ṣūrat.

# غزل

بساطِ رقص پہ صد شرق و غرب سے سرِ شام
دمک رہا ہے تری دوستی کا ماہِ تمام
چھلک رہی ہے ترے حُسنِ مہرباں کی شراب
بھرا ہُوا ہے لبالب ہر اِک نگاہ کا جام
گلے میں تنگ ترے حرفِ لُطف کی باہیں
پسِ خیال کہیں ساعتِ سفر کا پیام

### *Song*

On the dancing-floor as evening
Approaches, from a hundred
Horizons east and westward
Your full-moon friendship shining—

The wine of your radiant kindness
Runs over, and every look
Is a cup brim-full, your gracious
Words clasp their arms round my neck—

Somewhere deep in my mind
The hour of departure lurks.

---

### *Song*

*On the dance-floor, as evening comes on, from a hundred easts and wests*
*The full moon of your friendship is glowing,*
*The wine of your gracious beauty is overflowing,*
*The cup of every glance is filled to the brim,*
*The arms of your winning words are fast round my neck;*
*Somewhere at the back of my thoughts is the message of the hour of the journey.*

---

### *G͟hazal*

Bisāt̤-e-raqṣ pĕ ṣad sharq-o-g͟harb se sar-e-shām
Damak-rahā hai tĕrī dostī kā māh-e-tamām,
Chhalak-rahī hai tĕre ḥusn-e-mĕhrbāṅ kī sharāb,
Bharā hū'ā hai labālab harĕk nigāh kā jām,
Gale meṅ taṅg tĕre ḥarf-e-lut̤f kī bāheṅ;
Pas-e-k͟hayāl kahīṅ sā'at-e-safar kā payām.

---

ابھی سے یاد میں ڈھلنے لگی ہے صُحبتِ شب
ہر ایک رُوئے حسیں ہو چلا ہے بیشِ حسیں
ملے کچھ ایسے، جُدا یوں ہُوئے کہ فیضؔ اب کے
جو دِل پہ نقش بنے گا وُہ گُل ہے داغ نہیں

Into memory this night's glowing
Fellowship starts to melt, still lovelier
All these lovely faces grow.

Such a meeting, such a parting,
Faiz, will leave no scar imprinted,
But a blossom, on the heart.

*Already the evening's company has begun to melt into memory,*
*Every lovely face is becoming more lovely.*
*We met in such a way, we separated so, Faiz, that now*
*The mark that will be made on the heart will be a flower, not a scar.*

Abhī se yād meṅ ḍhalne-lagī hai ṣuḥbat-e-shab,
Harek rū-e-ḥusīṅ ho-chalā hai besh ḥasīṅ.
Mile kuchh aise, judā yūṅ hū'e kĕ, Faiẓ, abke
Jo dil pĕ naqsh banegā vo gul hai dāg͟h nahīṅ.

# تنہائی

آج تنہائی کسی ہمدمِ دیریں کی طرح
کرنے آئی ہے مری ساقی گری شام ڈھلے
منتظر بیٹھے ہیں ہم دونوں کہ مہتاب ابھرے
اور ترا عکس جھلکنے لگے ہر سائے تلے

## 40. LONELINESS

Today loneliness like a well-tried friend
Has come to be my evening wine-pourer.
We sit together waiting for the moon to rise
And set your image gleaming in every shadow.

### *LONELINESS*

1 *Today loneliness like some old friend*
*Has come to do my wine-pouring as evening declines;*
*We two are seated waiting for the moon to rise,*
*And for your reflection to begin shining under every shadow.*

### TANHĀ'Ī

1 Āj tanhā'ī kisī hamdam-e-derīṅ kī ṯaraḥ
Karne ā'ī hai mĕrī sāqīgarī shām ḍhale;
Muntaẕir baiṭhe haiṅ ham donoṅ kĕ mahtāb ubhare,
Aur tĕrā 'aks jhalakne-lage har sā'e tale.

# شام

اِس طرح ہے کہ ہر اِک پیڑ کوئی مندِر ہے،
کوئی اُجڑا ہُوا، بے نُور پُرانا مندِر،
ڈھُونڈتا ہے جو خرابی کے بہانے کب سے
چاک ہر بام، ہر اِک در کا دمِ آخر ہے۔
آسماں کوئی پُروہِت ہے جو ہر بام تلے
جِسم پر راکھ ملے، ماتھے پہ سِیندُور ملے
سر نِگُوں بیٹھا ہے چُپ چاپ نہ جانے کب سے

اِس طرح ہے کہ پسِ پردہ کوئی ساحر ہے
جِس نے آفاق پہ پھیلایا ہے یُوں سِحر کا دام،

## 41. EVENING

It is as if each tree
Were an old deserted shrine,
Unlighted, long since pining
To be free to crumble away—
Each rooftop gaping, every
Portal at the last gasp;
And heaven a sort of priest,
Squatting since god knows when
Under the eaves, brow daubed
With scarlet, body with ashes,
Speechless, head hanging down,
—As if behind the curtain
There were some conjuror
Drawing such webs of magic
Over the universe,

### *EVENING*

*It is as if every tree is some temple,*
*Some ruined, unlit old temple,*
*Which since long is seeking excuses for crumbling;*
*Each roof torn, every door is at its last breath.*
*The sky is some priest who at the foot of each roof-wall,*
*On his body ashes smeared, on his forehead vermilion smeared,*
*Head drooping, is seated silent, there is no knowing since when.*

*It is as if behind the curtain there is some magician*
*Who has so spread over the heavens a net of magic,*

### SHĀM

Is ṭaraḥ hai kĕ harĕk peṛ ko'ī mandir hai,
Ko'ī ujṛā hū'ā, be-nūr purānā mandir,
Ḍhūṅḍtā hai jo k̲h̲arābī ke bahāne kab se;
Chāk har bām, harĕk dar kā dam-e-āk̲h̲ir hai.
Āsmāṅ ko'ī purohit hai jo har bām tale,
Jism par rākh male, māthe pĕ sīṅdūr male,
Sar nigūṅ baiṭhā hai chup-chāp na jāne kab se.

Is ṭaraḥ hai kĕ pas-e-parda ko'ī sāḥir hai
Jis-ne āfāq pĕ phailāyā hai yūṅ siḥr kā dām,

دامنِ وقت سے پیوست ہے یوں دامنِ شام،
اب کبھی شام بُجھے گی نہ اندھیرا ہو گا
اب کبھی رات ڈھلے گی نہ سویرا ہو گا

آسماں آس لیے ہے کہ یہ جادُو ٹُوٹے
چُپ کی زنجیر کٹے، وقت کا دامن چھُوٹے
دے کوئی سنکھ دُہائی، کوئی پایل بولے
کوئی بُت جاگے، کوئی سانولی گھُونگٹ کھولے

And time's skirt and this evening's
Were stitched together so close,
That twilight will never end,
Darkness will never come,
Night never decline, or morning
Ever return. . . . Heaven's prayer
Is that the spell may break,
The chain of silence snap,
Time's skirt be disentangled—
Some wailing conch-shell blare,
Some jingling anklet speak,
Some idol waken, or some
Swart votaress lift her veil.

*The evening's skirt is so joined with the skirt of time,*
*Now evening will never be extinguished and darkness never come,*
*Now night will never decline nor morning come.*

*Heaven has the hope that this spell may be broken,*
*That the chain of silence may be snapped, the skirt of time be freed,*
*That some conch-shell may make outcry, some anklet speak,*
*Some idol awaken, some swarthy-beauty open her veil.*

Dāman-e-waqt se paiwast hai yūṅ dāman-e-shām,
Ab kabhī shām bujhegī na aṅdherā hogā,
Ab kabhī rāt ḍhalegī na sawerā hogā.

Āsmāṅ ās liye hai kĕ ye jādū ṭūṭe,
Chup kī zaṅjīr kaṭe, waqt kā dāman chhūṭe,
De ko'ī saṅkh duhā'ī, ko'ī pāyal bole,
Ko'ī but jāge, ko'ī sāṅwalī ghūṅgaṭ khole.

# آج بازار میں پا بہ جولاں چلو

چشمِ نم، جانِ شوریدہ کافی نہیں
تہمتِ عشقِ پوشیدہ کافی نہیں
آج بازار میں پا بہ جولاں چلو
دست افشاں چلو، مست و رقصاں چلو
خاک بر سر چلو، خوں بہ داماں چلو
راہ تکتا ہے سب شہرِ جاناں، چلو

حاکمِ شہر بھی، مجمعِ عام بھی
تیرِ الزام بھی، سنگِ دشنام بھی
صبحِ ناشاد بھی، روزِ ناکام بھی

## 42. NOT ENOUGH

Not enough the tear-stained eye, the storm-tossed life,
Not enough the secret love, suspicion's brand;
Come today in fetters to the marketplace,
Walk with waving hands, run in a drunkard's dance,
Clothes besmeared with blood and head begrimed with dust!
All the loved one's city is watching by the road:
There the governor waits, and there the populace,
Calumny's keen arrow, insult's hurtling stone,
Morning of ill omen, day of evil chance—

### *TODAY COME IN FETTERS TO THE MARKETPLACE*

*The wet eye, the stormy spirit, are not enough,*
*The accusation of secret love is not enough:*
*Today come in fetters to the marketplace,*
*Come waving hands, come exulting, dancing,*
*Come with dust on the head, come with blood on the dress.*
*All the city of the beloved is gazing, come;*
*There too is the governor of the city, the public gathering too,*
*The arrow of calumny too, the stone of abuse too,*
*The unhappy daybreak too, the wretched day too.*

### ĀJ BĀZĀR MEṄ PĀ-BAJAULĀṄ CHALO

Chashm-e-nam, jān-e-shorīda kāfī naḥīṅ,
Tuhmat-e-'ishq-e-poshīda kāfī nahīṅ:
Āj bāzār meṅ pā-bajaulāṅ chalo,
Dast-afshāṅ chalo, mast o raqṣāṅ chalo,
Khāk bar sar chalo, khūṅ ba-dāmāṅ chalo.
Rāh-taktā hai sab shahr-e-jānāṅ, chalo;
Ḥākim-e-shahr bhī, majma'-e-'ām bhī,
Tīr-e-ilzām bhī, saṅg-e-dushnām bhī,
Ṣubḥ-e-ṅāshād bhī, roz-e-nākām bhī.

اِن کا دم ساز اپنے سوا کون ہے
شہرِ جاناں میں اب باصفا کون ہے
دستِ قاتل کے شایاں رہا کون ہے
رَختِ دِل باندھ لو دِل فگارو چلو
پھر ہمیں قتل ہو آئیں یارو چلو

Who has been their bosom friend, but we alone?
In the loved one's city who is left to trust?
Who is worthy now of the executioner's hand?
You that know affliction, lift the heart's sad load;
We it is, my friends, must once more taste the knife.

*Who is their intimate, besides us?*
*In the city of the beloved who now is pure,*
*Who is left worthy of the executioner's hand?*
*Fasten-on the burden of the heart, heart-afflicted ones, come;*
*Let us once again go to be murdered—friends, come.*

Inkā dam-sāz apne siwā kaun hai?
Shahr-e-jānāṅ meṅ ab bā-ṣafā kaun hai,
Dast-e-qātil ke shāyāṅ rahā kaun hai?
Rakht-e-dil bāṅdh-lo, dil-fagāro, chalo;
Phir hamīṅ qatl ho-ā'eṅ, yāro, chalo.

# قیدِ تنہائی

دُور آفاق پہ لہرائی کوئی نُور کی لہر
خواب ہی خواب میں بیدار ہُوا درد کا شہر
خواب ہی خواب میں بے تاب نظر ہونے لگی
عدم آبادِ جُدائی میں سحر ہونے لگی؛
کاسۂ دِل میں بھری اپنی صبُوحی مَیں نے
گھول کر تلخیِ دِیروز میں اِمروز کا زہر

دُور آفاق پہ لہرائی کوئی نُور کی لہر
آنکھ سے دُور کسی صُبح کی تمہید لیے

## 43. SOLITARY CONFINEMENT

Far on the horizon a tremor of light flickered.
Still plunged in sleep pain's citadel grew conscious,
Still plunged in sleep eyes grew once more restless;
Over the ghostly house of exile, dawn.
In my heart's cup I poured the morning draught,
Stirring in yesterday's gall today's poison.

Far on the horizon a tremor of light flickered,
Harbinger of a still invisible daybreak;

### *SOLITARY CONFINEMENT*

*Far away on the horizon some ripple of light rippled;*
*Still in sleep the city of pain came awake,*
*Still in sleep the eye began to be restless,*
*In separation's abode of non-existence it began to be morning;*
*In the cup of the heart I poured my morning-draught,*
*Mixing in the bitterness of yesterday the poison of today.*

*Far away on the horizon some ripple of light rippled,*
*Bringing a presage of some dawn far out of sight;*

### QAID-E-TANHĀ'Ī

Dūr āfāq pĕ lahrā'ī ko'ī nūr kī lahr;
Khẉāb hī khẉāb meṅ bedār hū'ā dard kā shahr,
Khẉāb hī khẉāb meṅ be-tāb naẓar hone-lagī,
'adam-ābād-e-judā'ī meṅ saḥar hone-lagī;
Kāsa-e-dil meṅ bharī apnī ṣabūḥī maiṅ-ne,
Gholkar talkhī-e-dīroz meṅ imroz kā zahr.

Dūr āfāq pĕ lahrā'ī ko'ī nūr kī lahr,
Āṅkh se dūr kisī ṣubḥ kī tamhīd liye;

کوئی نغمہ، کوئی خوشبو، کوئی کافر صورت
عدم آبادِ جدائی میں مسافر صورت
بے خبر گزری، پریشانیِ امّید لیے-
گھول کر تلخیِ دیروز میں امروز کا زہر
حسرتِ روزِ ملاقات رقم کی میں نے
دیس پردیس کے یارانِ قدح خوار کے نام
حسنِ آفاق، جمالِ لب و رخسار کے نام

Some melody, some perfume, some siren face.
Strayed like a careless passer-by through the ghostly
House of exile, bringing all hope's torment.

Stirring in yesterday's gall today's poison
I made an offering of my homesickness
To friends in this and all lands who have drunk with me,
To earth's beauty, to the charm of cheek and lip.

*Some song, some scent, some sinfully-beguiling face,*
*In separation's abode of non-existence a roving face*
*Carelessly passed, bringing the anguish of hope.*
*Mixing in the bitterness of yesterday the poison of today,*
*I dedicated my aching for the day of meeting*
*To cup-drinking friends in this country and abroad,*
*To the beauty of the world, to the fairness of lip and cheek.*

Ko'ī naghma, ko'ī khwushbū, ko'ī kāfir ṣūrat,
'adam-ābād-e-judā'ī meṅ musāfir ṣūrat
Be-khabar guzrī, pareshānī-e-ummed liye.
Gholkar talkhī-e-dīroz meṅ imroz kā zahr,
Ḥasrat-e-roz-e-mulāqāt raqam kī maiṅ-ne
Des pardes ke yārān-e-qadaḥkhwār ke nām,
Ḥusn-e-āfāq, jamāl-e-lab-o-rukhsār ke nām.

# حمد

مِلکِ شہرِ زندگی تیرا
شُکر کِس طَور سے ادا کیجے
دَولتِ دِل کا کُچھ شُمار نہیں
تنگ دستی کا کیا گِلا کیجے

جو تِرے حُسن کے فقیر ہُوئے
اُن کو تشوِیشِ روزگار کہاں
دَرد بیچیں گے گیت گائیں گے
اِس سے خُوش وقت کاروبار کہاں

## 44. HYMN OF PRAISE

Sovereign lady of life's city,
How can our thanks to you be told?
Wealth the heart owns past all counting:
How then complain of penury?
Why should pensioners on your beauty
Take anxious thought for daily bread?
Making songs and selling sorrows—
Where should they find a merrier trade?

### *PRAISE*

*Queen of the city of life,*
*In what way could thanks to you be performed?*
*There is no counting up the wealth of the heart;*
*What complaint of poverty could be made?*
*Those who have become devotees of your beauty,*
*Where for them is anxiety about livelihood?*
*We shall sell pain, we shall sing songs—*
*Where a happier occupation than this?*

### ḤAMD

Malka-e-shahr-e-ziṅdagī, terā
Shukr kis ṭaur se adā kīje?
Daulat-e-dil kā kuchh shumār nahīṅ;
Taṅgdastī kā kyā gilā kīje?
Jo tĕre ḥusn ke faqīr hū'e,
Unko tashwīsh-e-rozgār kahāṅ?
Dard becheṅge, gīt gā'eṅge—
Is-se k͟hẉushwaqt kār-o-bār kahāṅ?

جام چھلکا تو جم گئی محفل
مِنّتِ لُطفِ غمِ گُسار کِسے
اشک ٹپکا تو کھِل گیا گُلشن
رنّجِ کم ظرفیِ بہار کِسے

خُوش نشیں ہیں کہ چشم و دِل کی مُراد
دَیر میں ہے نہ خانقاہ میں ہے
ہم کہاں قسمت آزمانے جائیں
ہر صنم اپنی بارگاہ میں ہے

کَون ایسا غنی ہے جِس سے کوئی
نقدِ شمس و قمر کی بات کرے
جِس کو شوقِ نبرد ہو ہم سے
جائے تسخیرِ کائنات کرے

When cups spill and guests are gathered,
  Who feels his debt to the comforter?
When tears fall the garden blossoms:
  Who bears a grudge at niggard Springs?
We are blest—no shrine, no temple,
  Shuts up from us our heart's desire;
Where should we go seeking fortune,
  When all we care for shares our roof?
Who is rich enough to chaffer
  About the moon and sun with us?
He who thirsts to give us battle
  May conquer first the universe.

*When the cup has overflowed the gathering has collected:*
*Who feels obligation to the graciousness of the consoler?*
*When the tear has spilled the flower-garden has bloomed:*
*Who feels grief at the inadequacy of spring?*
*We are fortunate that the desire of (our) eye and heart*
*Is neither in (Hindu) temple nor in (Muslim) shrine.*
*Where are we to go to test our fortune?*
*Every idol (attraction) is in our own mansion.*
*Who is rich enough to*
*Negotiate with us the price of the sun and moon?*
*Whoever has a wish for battle with us,*
*Let him go and make conquest of the universe.*

Jām chhalkā to j̣am-ga'ī maḥfil:
Minnat-e-lut̤f-e-ghamgusār kise?
Ashk ṭapkā to khil-gayā gulshan:
Raṅj-e-kamz̤arfī-e-bahār kise?
Khẉush-nashīṅ haiṅ kĕ chashm o dil kī ṃurād
Dair meṅ hai na khānqāh meṅ hai.
Ham kahāṅ qismat āzmāne jā'eṅ?
Har ṣanam apnī bārgāh meṅ hai.
Kaun aisā ghanī hai jis-se ko'ī
Naqd-e-shams-o-qamar kī bāt kare?
Jis-ko shauq-e-nabard ko ham-se,
Jā'e, taskhīr-e-kā'ināt kare.

# ڈھلتی ہے موجِ مے

ڈھلتی ہے موجِ مے کی طرح رات اِن دِنوں
کِھلتی ہے صُبح گُل کی طرح رنگ و بُو سے پُر
وِیراں ہیں جام، پاس کرو کچھ بہار کا
دِل آرزُو سے پُر کرو، آنکھیں لہُو سے پُر

## 45. LIKE FLOWING WINE

Night at this season comes on like flowing wine;
Dawn unfolds like a rose, all colour and scent.
If dust has filled the cup, pay honour to Spring—
With longing fill your heart, your eyes with fire.

## *FLOWS LIKE A WAVE OF WINE*

1 *Night flows these days like a wave of wine,*
*Dawn opens like a rose full of colour and scent;*
*If cups are desolate, have some respect for spring:*
*Fill the heart with desire, the eyes with blood.*

## ḌHALTĪ HAI MAUJ-E-MAI

1 Ḍhaltī hai mauj-e-mai kī t̤araḥ rāt in dinoṅ,
Khiltī hai ṣubḥ gul kī t̤araḥ raṅg o bū se pur;
Vīrāṅ haiṅ jām, pās karo kuchh bahār kā:
Dil ārzū se pur karo, āṅkheṅ lahū se pur.

# مُلاقات مِری

ساری دِیوار سِیَہ ہو گئی تا حلقۂ بام
راستے بُجھ گئے، رُخصت ہُوئے رہ گیر تمام
اپنی تنہائی سے گویا ہُوئی پھر رات مِری
ہو نہ ہو آج پھر آئی ہے مُلاقات مِری:
اِک ہتھیلی پہ حِنا، ایک ہتھیلی پہ لہُو
اِک نظر زہر لیے، ایک نظر میں دارُو

## 46. MY VISITOR

The whole wall has grown dim, to the circling roof;
All roads are blotted out, each wayfarer
Has taken his departure. Once again
My night and its own loneliness converse;
Once more my visitor I think has come,
This palm with henna stained, that palm with blood,
One glance all bane, the next all healing balm.

### *MY 'INTERVIEW'*

*All the wall has become black, up to the circle of the roof,*
*Roads have been extinguished, all travellers have taken leave;*
*My night has again begun talking with its solitude;*
*It seems that today my 'interview' has come again,*
*On one palm henna, on one palm blood,*
*One eye full of poison, in one eye medicine.*

### MULĀQĀT MĔRĪ

Sārī dīwār siya ho-ga'ī tā ḥalqa-e-bām,
Rāste bujh-ga'e, rukhṣat hū'e rah-gīr tamām;
Apnī tanhā'ī se goyā hū'ī phir rāt mĕrī;
Ho na ho āj phir ā'ī hai mulāqāt mĕrī,
Ĕk hathelī pĕ ḥinā, ek hathelī pĕ lahū,
Ĕk naẓar zahr liye, ek naẓar meṅ dārū.

دیر سے منزلِ دِل میں کوئی آیا نہ گیا
فُرقتِ درد میں بے آب ہُوا تختۂ داغ
کِس سے کہیے کہ بھرے رنگ سے زخموں کے ایاغ؛
اَور پھِر خُود ہی چلی آئی مُلاقات مِری،
آشنا موت جو دُشمن بھی ہے غم خوار بھی ہے
وُہ جو ہم لوگوں کی قاتل بھی ہے دِلدار بھی ہے

In my heart's lodging no-one now for long
Has come or gone; grey solitude has left
The garden of pain unwatered; who is there
To fill its chalices of wounds with crimson?

Once more indeed my visitor has come,
Of her own will, my old acquaintance Death,
She who is adversary and comforter both,
To such as us the murderess and the sweetheart.

*Since long no-one has come or gone in the halting-place of the heart;*
*In the isolation of pain the flowerbed of the scar has been unwatered—*
*Whom to tell that he should fill the cups of its wounds with colour?*
*And again of her own accord my 'interview' has come,*
*Familiar death, who is both enemy and grief-soother,*
*Who for us people is both murderess and sweetheart.*

Der se manzil-e-dil meṅ ko'ī āyā na gayā,
Furqat-e-dard meṅ be-āb hū'ā takhta-e-dāgh:
Kis-se kahiye kĕ bhare raṅg se zakhmoṅ ke ayāgh?
Aur phir khẉud-hī chalī ā'ī mulāqāt mĕrī,
Āshnā maut jo dushman bhī hai, ghamkhẉār bhī hai,
Vo jo ham logoṅ kī qātil bhī hai, dildār bhī hai.

# ختم ہوئی بارشِ سنگ

ناگہاں آج مرے تارِ نظر سے کٹ کر
ٹکڑے ٹکڑے ہوئے آفاق پہ خورشید و قمر
اب کسی سمت اندھیرا نہ اُجالا ہو گا
بجھ گئی دل کی طرح راہِ وفا میرے بعد
دوستو! قافلۂ درد کا اب کیا ہو گا

## 47. THE HAIL OF STONES

Suddenly pierced today by the sharp lance of my gaze
Moon and sun broke at once into fragments in the sky.

Now there will be no light nor darkness anywhere;
Now I am gone the pilgrim way lies hushed as my heart:
What will become of that band vowed to love's martyrdom?

### *THE RAIN OF STONES HAS ENDED*

*Suddenly today cut by the string of my glance*
*Sun and moon broke into pieces in the firmament.*
*Now there will not be darkness or brightness in any direction;*
*After me the way of fidelity has been extinguished like a heart;*
*Friends! what will become now of the caravan of pain (anguished love)?*

### K̲H̲ATM HŪ' Ī BARISH-E-SAṄG

Nāgahāṅ āj mĕre tār-e-naz̤ar se katkar
Ṭukṛe ṭukṛe hū'e āfāq pĕ k̲h̲ẉurshīd o qamar.
Ab kisī simt aṅdherā na ujālā hogā;
Bujh-ga'ī dil kī t̤araḥ rāh-e-wafā mere ba'd;
Dosto! qāfila-e-dard kā ab kyā hogā?

اب کوئی اَور کرے پرورشِ گُلشنِ غم
دوستو! ختم ہُوئی دِیدۂ تر کی شبنم:
تھم گیا شورِ جُنوں ختم ہُوئی بارشِ سنگ
خاکِ رہ آج لِئے ہے لبِ دِلدار کا رنگ:
کُوئے جاناں میں کُھلا میرے لہُو کا پرچم
دیکھئے دیتے ہیں کِس کِس کو صدا میرے بعد:
"کَون ہوتا ہے حرِیفِ مئے مَرد افگنِ عشق
ہے مُکرّر لبِ ساقی پہ صلا میرے بعد"

Some other now must tend the garden of sacrifice;
The dew these eyes of mine have shed, friends, is used up,
The passionate faith is stilled, the hail of stones is over.

Dust underfoot today is the hue of the loved one's lips,
In her dear street is unfurled the pennant of my blood.
To whom, whom will the summons come, now I am gone—
Who dares the challenge now of the deadly wine of love?
Again and again, now I am gone, this cry on the lips of her who pours.

*Now let someone else do the nourishing of the garden of suffering.*
*Friends! the dew of the wet eye is finished;*
*The tumult of rapture (madness) has ceased, the rain of stones has ended.*
*The dust of the road today bears the colour of the darling's lip,*
*In the sweetheart's street the pennant of my blood has spread out.*
*See to whom, to whom, they give the call after me—*
*'Who is the challenger of the man-overthrowing wine of love?*
*Repeatedly the cry is on the lips of the Saqi after me.'*

Ab ko'ī aur kare parwarish-e-gulshan-e-gham.
Dosto! khatm hū'ī dīda-e-tar kī shabnam;
Tham-gayā shor-e-junūṅ, khatm hū'ī bārish-e-saṅg.
Khāk-e-rah āj liye hai lab-e-dildār kā raṅg,
Kū-e-jānāṅ meṅ khulā mere lahū kā parcham:
Dekhiye dete haiṅ kis kis-ko ṣadā mere ba'd—
'Kaun hotā hai ḥarīf-e-mai-e-mard-afgan-e-'ishq?
Hai mukarrar lab-e-sāqī pĕ ṣalā mere ba'd.'

# رنگ ہے دِل کا مرے

تُم نہ آئے تھے تو ہر چیز وہی تھی کہ جو ہے:
آسماں حدِّ نظر، راہ گُذر راہ گُذر، شیشۂ مے شیشۂ مے۔
اَور اب شیشۂ مے، راہ گُذر، رنگِ فلک،
رنگ ہے دِل کا مرے، خُونِ جگر ہونے تک:
چمپئی رنگ کبھی، راحتِ دِیدار کا رنگ،
سُرمئی رنگ کہ ہے ساعتِ بیزار کا رنگ،
زرد پتّوں کا، خس و خار کا رنگ،
سُرخ پھُولوں کا، دہکتے ہُوئے گلزار کا رنگ،

## 48. BEFORE YOU CAME

Before you came, all things were what they are—
The sky sight's boundary, the road a road,
The glass of wine a glass of wine; since then,
Road, wineglass, colour of heaven, all have taken
The hues of this heart ready to melt into blood—
Now golden, as the solace of meeting is,
Now grey, the livery of despondent hours,
Or tint of yellowed leaves, of garden trash,
Or scarlet petal, a flowerbed all ablaze:

### *IT IS THE COLOUR OF MY HEART*

*You had not come, then each thing was the same that it is:*
*The sky the frontier of sight, a road a road, a glass of wine a glass of wine;*
*And now a glass of wine, a road, the colour of heaven,*
*Are the colour of my heart, 'about to turn into blood of the liver':*
*A golden colour sometimes, the colour of the joy of meeting,*
*A greyish colour that is the colour of an insipid span-of-time,*
*The colour of yellow leaves, of sticks and straw,*
*The colour of red flowers, of a flaming flower-bed,*

### RAṄG HAI DIL KĀ MĔRE

Tum nā a'e the to har chīz vuhī thī kĕ jo hai:
Āsmāṅ ḥadd-e-naẓar, rāhguzar rāhguzar, shīsha-e-mai shīsha-e-mai;
Aur ab shīsha-e-mai, rāhguzar, raṅg-e-falak,
Raṅg hai dil kā mĕre, k̲h̲ūn-e-jigar hone tak:
Champa'ī raṅg kabhī, rāḥat-e-dīdār kā raṅg,
Surma'ī raṅg kĕ hai sā'at-e-bezār kā raṅg,
Zard patton kā, k̲h̲as-o-k̲h̲ār kā raṅg,
Surk̲h̲ phūloṅ kā, dahakte hū'e gulzār kā raṅg,

زہر کا رنگ، لہو رنگ، شبِ تار کا رنگ۔

آسماں، راہ گذر، شیشۂ مے:

کوئی بھیگا ہُوا دامن، کوئی دُکھتی ہُوئی رگ،

کوئی ہر لحظہ بدلتا ہُوا آئینہ ہے۔

اب جو آئے ہو تو ٹھہرو کہ کوئی رنگ، کوئی رُت، کوئی شے،

ایک جگہ پر ٹھہرے،

پھر سے اک بار ہر اِک چیز وہی ہو کہ جو ہے:

آسماں حدِّ نظر، راہ گذر راہ گذر، شیشۂ مے شیشۂ مے

Colour of poisoṅ, colour of blood, or shade
Of sable night. Sky, highroad, glass of wine—
The first, a tear-stained robe, the next a nerve
Aching, the last a mirror momently altering. . . .
Now you have come, stay here, and let some colour,
Some month, some anything, keep its own place,
And all things once again be their own selves,
The sky sight's bound, the road a road, wine wine.

*The colour of poison, blood-colour, the colour of dark night.*
*Sky, road, glass of wine—*
*One a (tear-) wetted skirt, one an aching vein,*
*One is a mirror every moment changing.*
*Now that you have come, stay, so that some colour, some season, some thing,*
*May stay in one place,*
*So that again each object may be the same that it is,*
*The sky the frontier of sight, a road a road, a glass of wine a glass of wine.*

Zahr kā raṅg, lahū raṅg, shab-e-tār kā raṅg.
Āsmāṅ, rāhguzar, shīsha-e-mai:
Ko'ī bhīgā hū'ā dāman, ko'ī dukhtī hū'ī rag,
Ko'ī har laḥẓa badaltā hū'ā ā'īna hai.
Ab jo ā'e ho to ṭhahro, kĕ ko'ī raṅg, ko'ī rut, ko'ī shai,
Ek jaga par ṭhahre,
Phir se ĕk bār harĕk chīz vuhī ho kĕ jo hai—
Āsmāṅ ḥadd-e-naẓar, rāhguzar rāhguzar, shīsha-e-mai shīsha-e-mai.

# پاس رہو

تُم مرے پاس رہو
میرے قاتل، مرے دِلدار، مرے پاس رہو۔
جِس گھڑی رات چلے
آسمانوں کا لہُو پی کے سِیَہ رات چلے
مرہمِ مُشک لیے، نشترِ الماس لیے
بَین کرتی ہُوئی، ہنستی ہُوئی، گاتی نِکلے
درد کے کاسنی پازیب بجاتی نِکلے؛
جِس گھڑی سینوں میں ڈُوبے ہُوئے دِل
آستینوں میں نِہاں ہاتھوں کی رہ تکنے لگیں
آس لیے؛

## 49. BE NEAR ME

Be near me—
My torment, my darling, be near me
That hour when the night comes,
Black night that has drunk heaven's blood comes
With salve of musk-perfume, with diamond-tipped lancet,
With wailing, with jesting, with music,
With grief like a clash of blue anklets—
When, hoping once more, hearts deep-sunk in men's bosoms
Wait, watch for the hands whose wide sleeves still
Enfold them,

### *BE NEAR ME*

*You be near me,*
*My destroyer, my sweetheart, be near me—*
*At the hour when night comes,*
*When dark night having drunk the blood of the heavens comes*
*Bearing the salve of musk, bearing the lancet of diamond,*
*Comes out making lamentation, laughing, singing,*
*Comes out sounding blue-grey anklets of pain;*
*At the hour when hearts sunk in breasts*
*Have begun to watch out for hands hidden in sleeves,*
*With hope,*

### PĀS RAHO

Tum mĕre pās raho,
Mere qātil, mĕre dildār, mĕre pās raho—
Jis ghaṛī rāt chale,
Āsmānoṅ kā lahū pīke siya rāt chale
Marham-e-mushk liye, nishtar-e-almās liye,
Bain kartī hū'ī, haṅstī hū'ī, gātī nikle,
Dard ke kāsnī pāzeb bajātī nikle;
Jis ghaṛī sīnoṅ meṅ ḍūbe hū'e dil
Āstīnoṅ meṅ nihāṅ hāthoṅ kī rah-takne lageṅ,
Ās liye;

اَور بچّوں کے بِلکنے کی طرح قُلقُلِ مَے

بَہرِ ناسُودگی مچلے تو منائے نہ مَنے،

جب کوئی بات بنائے نہ بنے

جب نہ کوئی بات چلے۔

جِس گھڑی رات چلے،

جِس گھڑی ماتمی، سُنسان، سِیَہ رات چلے،

پاس رہو،

میرے قاتِل، مرے دِلدار مرے پاس رہو

Till wine's gurgling sound is a sobbing of infants
Unsatisfied, fretful, no soothing will silence,—
No taking thought prospers,
No thought serves;
—That hour when the night comes,
That hour when black night, drear, forlorn, comes,
Be near me,
My torment, my darling, be near me!

*And gurgling of wine, like a sobbing of children,*
*Because of frustration is fractious, and though you may soothe it will not be soothed;*
*When whatever thing you try to bring about will not be brought about,*
*When nothing succeeds:*
*At the hour when night comes,*
*At the hour when mournful, dreary, black night comes,*
*Be near,*
*My destroyer, my sweetheart, be near me.*

Aur bachchoṅ ke bilakne kī ṭaraḥ qulqul-e-mai
Bahr-e-nāsūdgī machle to manā'e na mane;
Jab ko'ī bāt banā'e na bane,
Jab na ko'ī bāt chale:
Jis ghaṛī rāt chale,
Jis ghaṛī mātamī, sunsān, siya rāt chale,
Pās raho,
Mere qātil, mĕre dildār, mĕre pās raho.

# منظر

رہ گُذر، سائے، شجر، منزلِ و در، حلقۂ بام،
بام پر سینۂ مہتاب کھُلا آہستہ
جس طرح کھولے کوئی بندِ قبا آہستہ۔
حلقۂ بام تلے، سایوں کا ٹھہرا ہُوا نیل،
نیل کی جھیل،
جھیل میں چُپکے سے تیرا کسی پتّے کا حباب
ایک پل تیرا، چلا، پھُوٹ گیا آہستہ

## 50. AN IDYLL

Shadows and road—trees, dwellings, doors—rim of the roof;
High on the roof softly the moon baring her breast,
Like a clasped gown softly unloosed;
Under the eaves motionless blue
Shades, a blue pool:
Noiseless, a leaf, soft as a brief bubble that bursts,
Drifting across.

## *A SCENE*

*Road, shadows, trees, houses and doors, edge of the roof—*
*Over the roof the bosom of the moon was opened softly*
*As if someone were undoing the fastening of a dress softly;*
*Below the edge of the roof, a stagnant blue of shadows,*
*A lake of blue;*
*In the lake silently floated some leaf, like a bubble,*
*One moment floated, moved, burst (vanished) softly.*

## MANZ̤AR

Rahguzar, sā'e, shajar, manzil-o-dar, ḥalqa-e-bām—
Bām par sīna-e-mahtāb khulā āhista,
Jis ṭaraḥ khole ko'ī baṅd-e-qabā āhista;
Ḥalqa-e-bām tale sāyoṅ kā ṭhahrā hū'ā nīl,
Nīl kī jhīl;
Jhīl meṅ chupke-se tairā kisī patte kā ḥabāb,
Ek pal tairā, chalā, phūṭ-gayā āhista.

بہُت آہستہ، بہُت ہلکا، خُنک رنگِ شراب
میرے شیشے میں ڈھلا آہستہ؛
شیشہ و جام، صُراحی، ترے ہاتھوں کے گُلاب
جس طرح دُور کسی خواب کا نقش
آپ ہی آپ بنا، اور مِٹا آہستہ

دِل نے دُہرایا کوئی حرفِ وفا آہستہ
تُم نے کہا "آہستہ!"
چاند نے جُھک کے کہا:
"اور ذرا آہستہ!"

Pale, very pale, slow, very slow, cool-coloured wine
Softly was poured into my glass;
Flagon and glass, rose of your hands,
Formed like a dream image far off,
Formed of themselves, softly dissolved.
Softly my heart once and again murmured some pledge;
'Softly', you said—
'Softer!' the moon, leaning down, breathed.

*Very softly, very pale, a cool colour that was wine*
*Was poured out into my glass softly;*
*Glass and bowl, flagon, the rose of your hands,*
*Like the image of some distant dream,*
*Took shape of itself, and faded softly.*

*My heart repeated some word of fidelity, softly—*
*You said 'Softly!'*
*The moon, bending, said:*
*'A little more softly even!'*

Bahut āhista, bahut halkā, khunak raṅg-e-sharāb
Mere shīshe meṅ ḍhalā āhista;
Shīsha o jām, ṣurāḥī, tĕre hāthoṅ ke gulāb
Jis ṭaraḥ dūr kisī khẉāb kā naqsh
Āp hī āp banā, aur miṭā āhista.

Dil-ne duhrāyā ko'ī ḥarf-e-wafā āhista—
Tum-ne kahā 'Āhista!'
Chāṅd-ne jhukke kahā:
'Aur ẕarā āhista!'

# غیر مُدوّن منظُومات

# UNCOLLECTED POEMS

## *UNCOLLECTED POEMS*

## GHAIR-MUDAWWAN MANẒŪMĀT

# گِیت

دَرد تھم جائے گا، غم نہ کر، غم نہ کر
یار لَوٹ آئیں گے، دِل ٹھہر جائے گا، غم نہ کر، غم نہ کر
زخم بھر جائے گا، غم نہ کر، غم نہ کر
دِن نِکل آئے گا، غم نہ کر، غم نہ کر
اَبر کُھل جائے گا، رات ڈھل جائے گی، غم نہ کر، غم نہ کر
رُت بدل جائے گی، غم نہ کر، غم نہ کر

## 51. SONG

The pain will end—do not wail,
Do not weep or wail!
Friends will come back, the heart be at rest,
Do not wail—
The wound will mend,
The day will dawn—do not wail!
Clouds will scatter and darkness fail,
The season will change—do not weep or wail!

## *SONG*

*Pain will cease, do not grieve, do not grieve—*
*Friends will return, the heart will rest, do not grieve, do not grieve—*
*The wound will be made whole, do not grieve, do not grieve—*
*Day will come forth, do not grieve, do not grieve—*
*The cloud will open, night will decline, do not grieve, do not grieve—*
*The season will change, do not grieve, do not grieve.*

## GĪT

Dard tham-jā'egā, g̲h̲am na kar, g̲h̲am na kar—
Yār lauṭ-ā'eṅge, dil ṭhahar-jā'egā, g̲h̲am na kar, g̲h̲am na kar—
Zak̲h̲m bhar-jā'egā, g̲h̲am na kar, g̲h̲am na kar—
Din nikal-ā'egā, g̲h̲am na kar, g̲h̲am na kar—
Abr khul-jā'egā, rāt ḍhal-jā'egī, g̲h̲am na kar, g̲h̲am na kar—
Rut badal-jā'egī, g̲h̲am na kar, g̲h̲am na kar.

# بلیک آؤٹ

جب سے بے نُور ہُوئی ہیں شمعیں
خاک میں ڈھُونڈتا پھِرتا ہُوں، نہ جانے کس جا
کھو گئی ہیں مری دونوں آنکھیں،
تُم جو واقف ہو بتاؤ کوئی پہچان مری۔
اِس طرح ہے کہ ہر اِک رگ میں اُتر آیا ہے
مَوج در مَوج کسی زہر کا قاتل دریا؛
تیرا ارمان تری یاد لیے، جان مری،
جانے کس مَوج میں غلطاں ہے کہاں، دِل میرا؟
ایک پل ٹھیرو کہ اُس پار کسی دُنیا سے
برق آئے مری جانب یدِ بیضا لے کر

## 52. 'BLACK-OUT'

Since all the lamps went out
I have been groping in the dust, not knowing
Where are my eyes.
You that know, tell me what I am!
It feels as though some deadly flood of poison
Has poured, surge upon surge, through every vein,
Sweeping with it my memories of you, love, my longings;
How can I tell in what wave my heart is engulfed?
Be patient awhile, until from some world beyond
A lightning-flash approaches with dazzling hand

### *'BLACK-OUT'*

*Since the lamps have been without light,*
*I am seeking, moving about, in the dust: I do not know where*
*Both my eyes have been lost;*
*You who are familiar with me, tell me some identification of myself.*
*It is as if into every vein has descended,*
*Wave on wave, the murderous river of some poison,*
*Carrying longing for you, memory of you, my love;*
*How to know where, in what wave, my heart is swallowed?*
*Wait one moment, till from some world beyond*
*Lightning comes towards me with bright hand.*

### *BLACK-OUT*

Jab se be-nūr hū'ī haiṅ shamʿeṅ
K͟hāk meṅ ḍhūṅḍtā phirtā hūṅ, na jāne kis jā,
Kho-ga'ī haiṅ mĕrī donoṅ āṅkheṅ;
Tum jo wāqif ho batāo ko'ī pahchān mĕrī.
Is ṭaraḥ hai kĕ harĕk rag meṅ utar-āyā hai
Mauj dar mauj kisī zahr kā qātil daryā,
Terā armān tĕrī yād liye, jān mĕrī;
Jāne kis mauj meṅ g͟halṭāṅ hai kahāṅ dil merā?
Ek pal ṭhairo kĕ us-pār kisī dunyā se
Barq ā'e mĕrī jānib yad-e-beẓā lekar,

اور مری آنکھوں کے گُم گشتہ گُہر
جامِ ظُلمت سے سِیَہ مست نئی آنکھوں کے شب تاب گُہر
لَوٹا دے۔
ایک پل ٹھیرو کہ دَریا کا کہیں پاٹ لگے
اور نیا دِل میرا
زہر میں دُھل کے، فنا ہو کے، کِسی گھاٹ لگے!
پھِر پئے نذرِ نئے دِیدہ و دِل لے کے چلُوں
حُسن کی مدح کروں، شَوق کا مضمُوں لِکھّوں

And for the lost gems of my eyes
Brings new ones, shining, drunk
With shadows from the cup of night.
Be patient awhile till the torrent finds its banks,
And my heart renewed after knowing annihilation,
Washed pure with poison, finds some landing-place;
Then let me come with tribute of new heart-vision,
Speak beauty's praise, and write the meaning of love.

*And the lost pearls of my eyes,*
*As luminous pearls of new eyes drunk with the cup of darkness,*
*Restores.*
*Wait one moment till somewhere the breadth of the river is found,*
*And, renewed, my heart,*
*Having been washed in poison, having been annihilated, finds some landing-place;*
*Then let me come bringing, by way of offering, new sight and heart,*
*Let me make the praise of beauty, let me write of the theme of love.*

Aur mĕrī āṅkhoṅ kĕ gum-gashta guhar,
Jām-e-z̤ulmat se siyamast na'ī āṅkhoṅ ke shabtāb guhar,
Lauṭa-de.
Ek pal ṭhairo kĕ daryā kā kahīṅ pāṭ lage,
Aur nayā dil merā
Zahr meṅ ḍhulke, fanā hoke, kisī ghāṭ lage;
Phir pa'e naẕr na'e dīda o dil leke chalūṅ,
Ḥusn kī madḥ karūṅ, shauq kā maẓmūṅ likkhūṅ.

# ہارٹ اٹیک

درد اِتنا تھا کہ اُس رات دلِ وحشی نے
ہر رگِ جاں سے اُلجھنا چاہا،
ہر بُنِ مُو سے ٹپکنا چاہا؛
اَور کہیں دُور، ترے صحنِ چمن میں گویا
پتّا پتّا مِرے افسُردہ لہُو میں دُھل کر
حُسنِ مہتاب سے آزُردہ نظر آنے لگا؛
میرے وِیرانۂ تن میں گویا
سارے دُکھتے ہُوئے ریشوں کی طنابیں کُھل کر
سِلسِلہ وار پتا دینے لگیں
رُخصتِ قافلۂ شوق کی تیّاری کا؛

## 53. HEART-ATTACK

There was such pain that night my maddened spirit
Was on fire to wrestle with every living fibre,
Gush out through every pore.
It seemed as if far off in your green bower
The leaves all dripping with my agonized blood
Were sickening of the moon's beauty—
As if this body were a desert,
All these racked nerves its tent-ropes,
One after one slackening, warning
Of life's caravan making ready for departure.

### *'HEART-ATTACK'*

*The pain was such that that night my wild heart*
*Wanted to wrestle with every vein of life,*
*Wanted to drip away through every hair's root;*
*And somewhere far off (it was) as if in your garden courtyard*
*Every leaf, washed in my miserable blood,*
*Began to look weary of the moon's beauty;*
*As if in the desert of my body*
*The tent-ropes of all my aching nerves had loosened*
*And begun one after the other to give notice*
*Of preparation for the departure of the caravan of zest-of-living;*

### *HEART-ATTACK*

Dard itnā thā kĕ us rāt dil-e-vaḥshī-ne
Har rag-e-jāṅ se ulajhnā chāhā,
Har bun-e-mū se ṭapaknā chāhā;
Aur kahīṅ dūr, tĕre ṣaḥn-e-chaman meṅ goyā
Pattā pattā mĕre afsurda lahū meṅ ḍhulkar
Ḥusn-e-mahtāb se āzurda naz̤ar āne-lagā;
Mere vīrāna-e-tan meṅ goyā
Sāre dukhte hū'e reshoṅ kī t̤anābeṅ khulkar
Silsila-wār patā dene-lagīṅ
Ruk̲h̲ṣat-e-qāfila-e-shauq kī taiyārī kā;

اَور جب یاد کی بُجھتی ہُوئی شمعوں میں نظر آیا کہیں
ایک پل، آخری لمحہ تِری دِلداری کا،
دَرد اِتنا تھا کہ اُس سے بھی گُذرنا چاہا
ہم نے چاہا بھی، مگر دِل نہ ٹھہرنا چاہا

Somewhere in memory's dying candle-light
A momentary vision, last glimpse of your tenderness;
But even that, there was so much pain, I wanted to be done with
—Or *I* wanted to stay, but my spirit would not.

*And when in memory's expiring candles came in view somewhere*
*For one instant the final moment of your loving-kindness,*
*The pain was such that one wanted to pass by even it—*
*I indeed wished, but my heart did not wish, to stay.*

Aur jab yād kī bujhtī hū'ī sham'oṅ meṅ naẓar āyā kahīṅ
Ek pal, ākhirī lamḥa tĕrī dildārī kā,
Dard itnā thā kĕ us-se bhī guzarnā chāhā—
Ham-ne chāhā bhī, magar dil na ṭhahrnā chāhā.

# دُعا

آئیے ہاتھ اُٹھائیں ہم بھی،
ہم جنھیں رسمِ دُعا یاد نہیں،
ہم جنھیں سوزِ محبّت کے سوا
کوئی بُت، کوئی خُدا یاد نہیں۔
آئیے عرض گُزاریں کہ نگارِ ہستی
زہرِ اِمروز میں شیرینیِ فردا بھر دے؛
وُہ جنھیں تابِ گراں باریِ ایّام نہیں
اُن کی پلکوں پہ شب و روز کو ہلکا کر دے؛
جن کی آنکھوں کو رُخِ صُبح کا یارا بھی نہیں
اُن کی راتوں میں کوئی شمع مُنوّر کر دے؛

## 54. PRAYER

We for whom prayer is a custom forgotten,
We who except for love's flame
Know neither idol nor god—
Come, let us too lift our hands,
Make our petition that Life, our loved mistress,
Smooth today's venom with sweets of tomorrow—
Lighten on them that lack strength for its burden
Time, and the nights and the days—
Brighten with lamps in their darkness those eyes
Dawn's rosy face cannot touch!

### *PRAYER*

*Come, let us also lift our hands,*
*We who do not remember the custom of prayer,*
*We who, except for the burning fire of love,*
*Do not remember any idol, any god.*
*Come, let us present a petition that Life, our beloved,*
*Will pour tomorrow's sweetness into today's poison;*
*That for those who have not strength for the burden of the days,*
*May it make night and day (weigh) light on their eyelashes;*
*For those whose eyes have not strength for (seeing) the face of dawn,*
*May it light some candle in their nights;*

### DU'Ā

Ā'iye hāth uṭhā'eṅ ham bhī,
Ham jinheṅ rasm-e-du'ā yād nahīṅ,
Ham jinheṅ soz-e-maḥabbat ke siwā
Ko'ī but, ko'ī khudā yād nahīṅ.
Ā'iye 'arz guzāreṅ kĕ nigār-e-hastī
Zahr-e-imroz meṅ shīrīnī-e-fardā bhar-de;
Vo jinheṅ tāb-e-girāṅbārī-e-aiyām nahīṅ
Unkī palkoṅ pĕ shab o roz ko halkā kar-de;
Jin-kī āṅkhoṅ ko rukh-e-ṣubḥ kā yārā bhī nahīṅ
Unkī rātoṅ meṅ ko'ī sham' munavvar kar-de;

جن کے قدموں کو کسی رہ کا سہارا بھی نہیں
اُن کی نظروں پہ کوئی راہ اُجاگر کر دے؛
جن کا دیں پیرویِ کذب و ریا ہے، اُن کو
ہمّتِ کفر ملے، جُرأتِ تحقیق ملے؛
جن کے سر منتظرِ تیغِ جفا ہیں، اُن کو
دستِ قاتل کو جھٹک دینے کی توفیق ملے۔
عشق کا سرِّ نہاں جانِ تپاں ہے جس سے
آج اِقرار کریں اور تپش مٹ جائے؛
حرفِ حق دِل میں کھٹکتا ہے جو کانٹے کی طرح
آج اِقرار کریں، اور خلش مٹ جائے۔

May there be shown to those feet that no
Pathways have aided, some road—
May there be given to deceit's slavish votaries
Will to deny and to seek—
Courage, to men whose heads tyranny's
Sword hovers over, to fend off the murderous hand!

Love's hidden mystery—man's fevered soul: today let us
Make a new covenant with it, its fever be slaked;
Truth's potent word, that keeps pricking the heart like a
thorn,
Make it our own, and the throbbing pain bring to an end.

*For those for whose steps there is no assistance of any road,*
*May it make some road luminous to their sight;*
*To those whose religion is pursuit of lying and hypocrisy,*
*May there come courage for denial, resolution for truth;*
*To those whose heads are awaiting the sword of oppression,*
*May there come capacity to shake off the murderer's hand.*
*The hidden secret of love is the fevered soul, with which*
*Let us today make a covenant, and let its fever be slaked;*
*The word of Truth, which throbs in the heart like a thorn,*
*Let us today accept, and the anguish be wiped out.*

Jin-ke qadmoṅ ko kisī rah kā sahārā bhī nahīṅ
Unkī naẓroṅ pĕ ko'ī rāh ujāgar kar-de;
Jin-kā dīṅ pairavī-e-kiẕb-o-riyā hai, unko
Himmat-e-kufr mile, jur'at-e-taḥqīq mile;
Jin-ke sar muntaẓir-e-tegh-e-jafā haiṅ, unko
Dast-e-qātil ko jhaṭak-dene kī taufīq mile.
'ishq kā sirr-e-nihāṅ jān-e-tapāṅ hai jis-se
Āj iqrār kareṅ aur tapish miṭ-jā'e;
Ḥarf-e-ḥaq, dil meṅ khaṭaktā hai jo kāṅṭe kī ṭaraḥ,
Āj iqrār kareṅ, aur khalish miṭ-jā'e.

## NOTES ON THE INTRODUCTION

1. A Scotswoman who knew him in Afghanistan wrote in fictional form an admiring account of his efforts to establish order: see Lillias Hamilton, *A Vizier's Daughter* (London, 1900).
2. He is therefore, in full, Faiẓ Aḥmad 'Faiẓ'. His own name, religious like nearly all Muslim names, would mean 'Bounty of the Highly Praised One'—the Prophet. (He writes himself 'Aḥmed', not 'Aḥmad'.)
3. *The Observer* (London), March 11, 1951, in an article at the time of Faiz's first arrest.
4. In an article on 'Faiz and his Poetry' (in *New Age*, Delhi, April 1956) Sajjad Zaheer wrote: 'The writer of these lines was a co-accused with Faiz in this case . . . and he can testify to the high morale, the patriotic fervour, the serenity and the undaunted courage and faith in the high destiny of his beloved people which Faiz exemplified during this whole period.'
5. It is due to the late administration of President Ayyub Khan to state that Faiz's *Zindān-Nāma* ('Prison Thoughts') was written before its term of office; and that although he was known to be not in sympathy with this administration, the sponsoring of the present volume by Unesco was authorized by it, in recognition of his position as one of the country's most eminent writers.
6. Miss Achla Chib (now Mrs Eccles).
7. This is the view of Mr M. Usman, lecturer in Urdu at Government College, Lahore, who gave me much light on this and many other subjects when I was living in the College in 1965.
8. R. K. Yadav, *The Indian Language Problem* (Delhi, ? 1967), discusses the position of Urdu in Pakistan as well as in India.
9. Faiz expresses a degree of scepticism about the generalizations in this paragraph.
10. Faiz points out that the *kū-e-malāmat* might connote the worldling or the Pharisee, as well as the seeker of illicit pleasure.
11. See e.g. A. J. Arberry, *Sufism* (London, 1956); Khaliq Ahmad Nizami, *Some Aspects of Religion and Politics in India during the 13th Century* (Aligarh University, 1961).
12. My friend and former colleague Mr Kishan Singh, of the Panjabi College at Delhi, has given me valuable information about this folk-poetry, of which he has been a lifelong student.
13. Much Elizabethan sonneteering has a similar character. Cf. Professor Arberry's remark in his English edition of Iqbal's long poem *Javid-Nama* (p. 13) that 'Persian is a language almost ideally suited to deliberate vagueness'.
14. Mr R. Russell of the University of London has written a most illuminating essay, 'The Pursuit of the Urdu Ghazal' (in the American *Journal of Asian Studies*, November 1969). See also, by him and Khurshidul Islam, *Three Mughal Poets* (London, 1969), and *Ghalib*: Vol. 1, *Life and Letters* (London, 1969).
15. A number of Iqbal's *ghazals* will be found in my *Poems from Iqbal*.

16. See the poem 'Capital and Labour', in *Poems from Iqbal*, pp. 21–3.
17. See W. G. Archer, *Indian Painting in the Punjab Hills* (London, 1952), pp. 5, 39.
18. This point of contrast was stressed during a discussion by Mr S. N. Chib.
19. No. 113 in *Poems from Iqbal.*
20. Dr Nazir Ahmad, in a letter of August 20, 1967. The same critic however has found occasional phrases of Faiz to be in very unorthodox Urdu. (Examples, for the student: no. 38, line 17; no. 52, line 14.)

## NOTES ON THE POEMS

**(The numbers below are those of poems in this collection; numbers in brackets refer to lines, in the original text and transliteration.)**

*Naqsh-e-Faryādī*. This untranslatable title comes from the opening of Ghalib's Urdu poems, where instead of the conventional expression of gratitude to God the poet says that all created things are protesting against their creator.

8 (6) The 'alien dust' is an oblique allusion to the withering touch of imperialism; cf. the recurrence of the word *ajnabī* (alien), with a more overtly political reference, in line 14 of the next poem.

9 This was a favourite poem at college *mushā'iras;* to student audiences its blend of patriotic and romantic had a special appeal. The verse translation is in approximately the metre of the original.

10 The opening couplet parodies that of a poem of Iqbal, 'The Prayer of Tariq'—the Muslim conqueror of Spain. Iqbal's warriors of the faith are endowed with zeal for religion (*ẕauq-e- k͟hudā'ī*), Faiz's mongrels with zeal for cadging (*ẕauq-e-gadā'ī*).

11 This poem made a great impression by its extreme simplicity and directness, though its style has seldom been reproduced since, either by imitators or by Faiz himself. The metre and rhyme-scheme of the verse translation are close to those of the original.

14 The situation referred to is that of the August rising of 1942 in India, though more than one interpretation is possible. The sonnet-form used in the translation seems not inappropriate. I once pointed out to Faiz that several of his poems were in fourteen lines, and asked whether they had been influenced by the sonnet; he said this might have happened without his being conscious of it, but fourteen lines happened to suit several of his rhyme-patterns.

15 (4) The two worlds are that of sense, and the other, invisible one.

15 (8) *Parda-e-sāz* is a musical term, for note or key, so that there is a kind of double meaning here.

*Dast-e-Ṣabā*. *Ṣabā* is any light breeze, particularly of early morning; it recurs frequently in these poems, and may be said to symbolize both a prisoner's tenuous contact with the free world outside, and mankind's hopes of liberation.

17 One of several poems that Faiz composed in solitary confinement, when deprived of writing materials, and was only able to write down several months later.

17 (1) *Lauḥ-o-qalam* is an instance of a religious memory woven into a new context, as not infrequently with Faiz. Traditionally the phrase relates to the Book of Destiny where all that was to happen was written down before the creation of the world. For Faiz, who uses it several times in poems of this

period (it forms the title of no. 20), it seems to symbolize the artist's endowment and his responsibility to his fellow-men.

18 The verse translation follows the *ghazal* form of the original, and its metre, except that its four feet (of five syllables each) are reduced to three.

18 (2) Faiz says that this line relates to recollections of youthful hope, with frustration and fulfilment alternating. But the whole poem is enigmatic and elusive.

18 (9–10) The antithesis of *rind* and *muḥtasib*, rake and official censor of morals, is traditional, with a frequent insinuation that the latter is a hypocrite, no better in reality than the former. Possibly this couplet is linked to the previous ones by an implied suggestion that sinner and puritan are equally fascinated by the lady with whom the poet is in love.

20 (3–4) Conventionally what lends the world vitality is love, or—virtually identical with it—the *pain* of love. The poet will keep inspiring men with the things (*asbāb*) that cause or constitute love and prevent the world from withering into a desert.

20 (9–10) An example of old symbols adapted to new meanings. The tavern and its wine stand for genuine religious feeling, the *ḥaram* or shrine for formal, perfunctory belief; here they suggest political idealism in contrast with soulless bureaucracy, and the *ṣanam* of line 12—idol, or mistress—is the People.

23 The poem was originally entitled 'Two Voices'. The metre of the verse translation is close to that of the Urdu, which except in the third stanza is in rhymed couplets like the translation.

23 (28) *Nuṭq*, 'mind', might also be rendered as 'the faculty of speech'.

23 (30) Kai: Khosrau, the ancient Persian king.

25 Written in solitary confinement in the spring of 1951, when Faiz was awaiting trial and there was reason to fear the worst.

25 (14) *Jabr* and *ikhtiyār* have the theological sense of necessity and free will; in this context they imply the alternative of slavish submission or revolt.

28 (5–6) Cool cloudy days and moonlit nights are the two times poetically regarded as appropriate to convivial parties, and therefore must awaken painful memories of friends one is cut off from.

30 Some revision of this poem has been made by Faiz for the present edition. It should be taken in a general sense, not as referring to any particular place or time.

31 The verse translation follows the *ghazal* form of the original.

31 (2) The opening of the buds is compared with the *chāk-e-girībāṅ*, the tearing of the garment from collar or breast downward, the traditional expression of unbearable emotion; cf. 13 (14).

31 (3–4) That is, signs of political progress could be observed here and there in the world. Asked about these signs, Faiz mentioned events in Persia, Egypt, Africa, and East Pakistan.

32 'May I be a sacrifice to—': a familiar expression of devotion, here ironical. Throughout this poem, as in various others, the poet uses the first person plural which may, as in Latin or Greek, denote either 'we' or 'I'. In this case he recommended that both words should figure in the translation, the idea being that one man is saying what many men are feeling.

32 (5–6) *Bast-o-kushād*, or 'administration', means literally 'closing and opening', and there is a punning allusion to a line of Sa'di where the same words refer to stones being kept shut up while dogs are turned loose. The point is that citizens are allowed no means of defending themselves against persecution.

32 (19 ff.) There are echoes here of Iqbal's poem *Maiṅ aur Tū* ('I and You'), in *Bāng-e-Darā*, with its allusion to the Quranic story, a favourite with Iqbal, of how Nimrod the tyrant, who pretended to be a god, tried to burn Abraham at the stake, and how the flames turned miraculously into flowers.

34 At the end of this poem Faiz writes, in the 1967 edition, *Nā-tamām*—'Unfinished'.

35 The city for whose familiar sights, so close to him yet invisible, the poet felt homesick, was old Lahore. He was brought here from Montgomery jail for a short time in the spring of 1954. The poem was begun at Lahore on March 28 and finished at Montgomery on April 15.

35 (14) *Lailas*, or 'sweethearts': Laila was the legendary lover of Majnun, and romantic love and political idealism are, as so often, equated.

36 Written in Montgomery jail in December 1954. The crosses or crucifixes of the poem are those formed by the grating of bars over the cell window. For Muslims, Jesus is a prophet and miracle-worker, but is not believed to have suffered the shameful humiliation of crucifixion. Faiz is the first Urdu poet to make an imaginative use of the idea of death on the cross.

37 Written in Montgomery jail on March 30, 1955. The original title was 'Africa Come Back'—a phrase that Faiz had heard of as the watchword of rebels in some part of Africa. A number of his poems have circulated in East Africa in Swahili versions.

*Dast-e-tah-e-Saṅg*—a forced promise; one makes a pledge by

putting one's hand in another's, but if the hand is trapped under a rock instead, no choice is left.

39 Impressions of a night at Urumchi in Sinkiang. The poem has a companion-piece called 'Peking'.

40 Written in April 1957.

41 A prison poem of 1956.

41 (5) I give the meaning as explained by Faiz, but the image, taken straightforwardly, is a curious one.

41 (6) The sacred marks on the forehead, and the smearing with ashes, belong to a Hindu holy man; and the closing lines evoke the morning ritual of a Hindu temple, with conch-shells blown to summon worshippers.

42 A poem in defence of patriots subjected to slander and misrepresentation.

44 (17–18) The wording is unusual; I give the meaning as explained by Faiz.

46 This and the next poem are coupled as 'Two Elegies' (*Do Marṣiye*); they were written in memory of a young progressive who perished in prison. He is imagined to be speaking in his own person. *Mulāqāt*—meeting, interview, visit—became a prisoners' term for a *visitor* allowed to see them.

47 (8) The madman pelted with stones by street urchins is a common poetical image.

47 (12–13) A quotation from Ghalib.

48 Written at Moscow, August 1963.

48 (4) *K͟hūn-e-jigar hone tak* is a phrase from Ghalib. The liver is associated with a more tender, affectionate kind of love than the heart.

49 Written at Moscow in 1963.

49 (12–13) There is an echo here, as so often, of Ghalib.

50 Written at Moscow in 1964. The recurrent word *āhista* usually means 'slowly', but may also mean 'softly': here, as Faiz pointed out to me, the two senses run into each other.

52 (10) *Yad-e-beẓā:* a phrase used of the miraculous shining of Moses's hand in the presence of Pharaoh.

52 (14) The wording is obscure; Faiz says it means: 'till the river finds its banks'—that is, I suppose, when the floodwater subsides and the banks re-emerge.

52 (16) *Fanā*, 'death' or 'destruction', was a term of the Sufi mystics for the total submergence of the conscious self in the infinite.

54 *Ḥamd*, 'praise', often signifies a hymn, or praise of God.

54 (19) There is an echo here of the last line but one of Iqbal's poem *Jabrīl o Iblīs* ('Gabriel and Satan'), in *Bāl-e-Jabrīl*, but with a transposition of meaning.

# INDEX OF FIRST LINES